POST-WAR RECONSTRUCTION IN FAILED STATES: THE CASE OF SIERRA LEONE

POST-WAR RECONSTRUCTION IN FAILED STATES: THE CASE OF SIERRA LEONE

ABDUL RAHMAN KAMARA

Flowers Publications
a Division of Flowers School of Technology and Management
Germany • United Kingdom

Kamara, Abdul Rahman

Post-War Reconstruction in Failed States: the Case of Sierra Leone | Abdul Rahman Kamara

ISBN-13: 978-1470177805 | ISBN-10: 1470177803

Post-war, Reconstruction, Failed States, Sierra Leone, Peace Studies, Conflicts.

Author url: www.arkamara.org

Dedicated to my wife Fatmata, son Edwin Akim and daughter Aaliyah Binta.

TABLE OF CONTENTS

ACKNOWLEDGMENTS

It is a pleasure to thank the many people who made this work possible. It is difficult to overstate my gratitude to my academic (MA and MPhil) supervisors, Professor Jenny Pearce and Dr Gary Little John. Without the assistance of Professor Pearce in explaining things clearly and simple this work would not have been possible. I also want to thank Professor David Francis with whose help I was able to finally complete the research work. A special thank you also goes to Michael Flowers. Throughout my research and thesis-writing period, he provided encouragement, sound advice and a lot of good ideas. I would have been lost without him.

I would like to thank all the people who taught me: Dr Betts Featherstone, Tom Woodhouse and Oliver Ramsbotham are to be named among others. A special thank you goes to John Meadley, Anne Holding and Professor Angela Kamara for their support.

I am indebted to my many student colleagues for providing a stimulating and fun environment in which to learn and grow. I am especially grateful to Ismail Oluwale, Sojie Adeneyie, John Kabia and Sahr Thomas.

I wish to thank my entire extended family for providing a loving environment for me. My siblings, and lastly, and most importantly, I wish to thank my Mother, Kissu Kamara-Sesay. She bore me, raised me, supported me, taught me, and loved me. To them I dedicate this work.

ABBREVIATIONS AND ACRONYMS

ACC	Anti-Corruption Commission
APC	All People's Congress
CGG	Campaign for Good Governance
CRP	Community Reintegration Project
CDF	Civil Defence Force
DfID	Department for International Development
DDR	Disarmament, Demobilisation and Reintegration
EU	European Union
EC/SLRRP	European Commission/Sierra Leone Resettlement and Rehabilitation Programme
ECOMOG	Economic Community of West African States Cease-Fire Monitoring Group
ECOWAS	Economic Community of West African States
EO	Executive Outcome
GoSL	Government of Sierra Leone
HQ	Headquarters
HRW	Human Rights Watch
ICG	International Crisis Group
IDP	Internally Displaced Person
IMATT	International Military Advisory and Training Team
IMF	International Monetary Fund
INGO	International Non-Governmental Organisation
MDTF	Multi-Donor Trust Fund
MOD	Ministry of Defence
NCDDR	National Committee for Disarmament, Demobilization and Reintegration
NCRRR	National Commission for Reconstruction, Resettlement and Rehabilitation
NGO	Non-Governmental Organisation
OWAP	Other War Affected People
PRA	Participatory Rural Appraisal
PRSP	Poverty Reduction Strategy Paper
PSO	Peace Support Operation
RSLAF	Republic of Sierra Leone Armed Forces
RUF	Revolutionary United Front
SLA	Sierra Leone Army
SILSEP	Sierra Leone Security Sector Reform Programme

SLP	Sierra Leone Police
SLPP	Sierra Leone People's Party
SSR	Security Sector Reform
TRC	Truth and Reconciliation Commission
TWP	Temporary Work Programme
UK	United Kingdom
UN	United Nations
UNAMSIL	United Nations Mission in Sierra Leone
UNDP	United Nations Development Programme
UNOMSIL	United Nations Observer Mission in Sierra Leone
UNPP	United National People's Party
WSB	West Side Boys

GLOSSARY

TEMNE: Temne is the second largest ethnic group in Sierra Leone. It comprises about 30 per cent of Sierra Leone's total population and can be found in the Western Atlantic Provinces of Sierra Leone. The history of the Temne people goes as far back as the late 15th or early 16th century, where they were apparently seeking access to new trade opportunities with the Portuguese who were trading along the Atlantic coast. At present, the Temne are involved in disputes over power with other large ethnic groups in Sierra Leone, particularly the Mende.

Sierra Leone's national politics centres on the competition between the North and the South of the country. The North is dominated by the Temne, and the South is dominated by the Mende. The latter are the former landlords of Freetown and also the tribe of the late rebel leader Colonel Foday Saybana Sankoh.

KRIO: Krio is an ethnic group in Sierra Leone, and its members are descendants of various groups of freed slaves from Nova Scotia, Jamaica and of re-captives from the high seas that landed in Freetown between 1787 and about 1855. The Krio speak a distinctive language, Krio, which is a Creole language based on English and African languages. They are mostly found in Freetown, on the Peninsula, on the Banana Islands, York Island and in the Bonthe district.

KAMAJORS: The Kamajors are traditional hunters from the Mende ethnic group in the southern and eastern regions of Sierra Leone who believe in supernatural and ancestral powers.

MENDE: The Mende are found in the southern and eastern parts of the country. They are the largest ethnic group comprising some 30 percent of the population.

LIMBA: The Limba predominate in 7 of Sierra Leone's 149 rural chiefdoms, and their community affairs are dominated by the local paramount chiefs. They are the third-largest tribe in the country and number about 350,000 (Alie 2004) Historical records indicate that the Limba ethnic group was among the last groups in Sierra Leone to seek Western education and contact with the outside world, and for many years they suffered from a negative public image due to their perceived 'backwardness.' Their position improved considerably, however, between 1968 and 1992, when two successive presidents of Sierra Leone (Siaka Stevens and Joseph Saidu Momoh) identified themselves as Limba. Major Johnny Paul Koroma, former leader of the Armed Forces Revolution Council, was also a Limba.

HOLISTIC: The term holistic may be defined as the tendency in nature to produce wholes from the orderly grouping of units, implying that the whole is greater than the sum of the parts and that all parts are important. This can be developed to mean an approach to reintegration that creates opportunity for all parties – and not just for some.

PREFACE

The purpose of this study is to understand the causes of the Sierra Leonean conflict and to analyse the reconstruction programmes that followed it. Post-war reconstruction programmes must not be limited to the re-joining of families or reintegration of communities. It must also go a long way in providing an improved situation for all those affected by the war. Notably, where post-war reconstruction programmes fail to focus on the original causes of the conflict, it may result in reinforcement of the original social structures and prejudices and in continued marginalisation of certain groups. Using post-conflict Sierra Leone as a case study, the study attempts to examine the notion that "post-war reconstruction programmes tend to reinforce earlier social structures and prejudices rather than create opportunities for the previously marginalised". The work focuses on the role of the Department for International Development (DfID)-funded Community Reintegration Programme (CRP). Considering the Sierra Leone post-war scenarios, the causes and political resolution of the conflict and the situation in 2001 when the conflict officially came to an end, the thesis reviews the philosophy, planning, policies, practices and activities of donor agencies in general and CRP in particular before assessing impact on the process of rebuilding communities in Sierra Leone.

INTRODUCTION

Bosnia, Angola, Cambodia, Liberia, Sierra Leone and other conflicts have posed challenges to peacemaking and policymaking agents alike, seeking to end such violent conflicts: How can the opposing warring factions be brought to a settlement? How has a peace agreement to be formulated to enhance a successful implementation thereof? How can the prospects of a stable peace be enhanced? One of the most challenging problems is the reassurance of the warring factions that the opposing party or parties will not renege the agreement. The security situation is most precarious immediately after the signing of a peace agreement, and there is a high risk of renewed hostilities. The successful implementation of a peace agreement lays the groundwork for a long-term peace-consolidating process to set in. A comprehensive peace agreement is a first step towards peace consolidation but it does not guarantee lasting stability as long as no mid- and long-term peace-consolidating measures have been put in place, which take into account and/or remove the underlying causes of the armed conflict.

The focus of this study lies on the post-war reconstruction phase of a peace process: Post-war reconstruction is the fragile stage of the peace process when war has ended but peace is not yet secure (Ramsbotham et al. 2005: 185). It can involve short-term tasks such as the demobilization and disarmament of the warring factions as well as mid- and long-term tasks such as rebuilding of state institutions and infrastructure, and reconciliation processes. Post-war reconstruction is especially challenging in a failed-state environment: the absence of a functioning state-apparatus has to be factored into the planning and implementation of the post-war reconstruction programmes. It implies that a traditional peacekeeping approach with a focus on the securing and monitoring of cease-fire provisions is not appropriate in dealing with a post-war reconstruction in a failed state.

In Chapter One, the concept of failed states is introduced with the emphasis on Sub-Saharan statehood. The literature review encompasses definitions of main terms concerning statehood and its failure, and Sub-Saharan statehood, and provides factors associated with state failure.

Chapter Two presents a theoretical framework that provides the basis for understanding the trends of civil wars and for the evaluation of peace processes. It seeks to systematically address aspects of conflict resolution from the causes to conflict management up to post-conflict reconstruction.

Chapter Three of the work seeks to explain the cause of Sierra Leone's conflict, addressing both the political history and economic factors leading to state failure, and presents an outline of the conflict and the attempts at conflict resolution, involving various actors. Viewing intrastate conflicts from a political economy perspective, for instance, can improve understanding of the key dynamics of a civil war. It can also lead to a more systematic understanding of how these dynamics impact on conflict resolution and post-conflict reconstruction.

Chapter Four focuses on the methodology of the research, including the outline of the research design, the relevance of the study and the chosen research method for the content analysis of the case study. The research methodology adopted a protocol approach to conducting interviews and distributing related questionnaires. Due to the sensitive nature of the civil war with respect badly victimised communities and or communities that played a vital role in the conflict, and considering the level of literacy, face-to-face interviews of representative communities and strategic groups were conducted in the key areas (northern and western) of Sierra Leone. Where appropriate, survey questionnaires were handed out. Target interviewee groups included planning donors, implementing and evaluating donors, strategic organisations, politicians, ex-combatants, internally displaced persons, community members and leaders, and security forces. In order to extract the emergent evaluative impressions and themes, a Content Analysis—a scholarly methodology used by researchers in the social sciences to analyse recorded transcripts of interviews with participants—was performed on the coded data based on 40 valid transcripts.

Chapter Five combines the theories and concepts presented in Chapter Two with the results of the field work conducted in Sierra Leone, focusing on the role of the DfID-funded Community Reintegration Programme (CRP) during post-war reconstruction.

The causative factors and the impact of DfID post-war reconstruction programmes in Sierra Leone are analysed in Chapter Six. The work rounds up with concluding comments and recommendations for further research.

The research work seeks to address the following questions in its analysis:

a. Why have post-war reconstruction programmes marginalised the poor?

b. To what extent is the civil war in Sierra Leone linked to national politics?

c. To what extent is the civil war in Sierra Leone linked to foreign influences?

d. What are the effects of the conflict on Sierra Leone's democratization process?

Answers to the research questions provide the basis for addressing the main hypothetical statement that: *donor-led post-war reconstruction programmes tend to reinforce earlier social structures and a return to the status quo rather than create opportunities for the previously marginalised.* Sierra Leone is used as a case study, and the role of the United Kingdom, including its Department for International Development and the British Army, in Sierra Leone's post-war reconstruction serves a specific focus of paramount interest.

LITERATURE REVIEW

RETHINKING SUB-SAHARAN STATEHOOD

1.1.   FAILED STATES IN CONTEXT

The concept 'failed states' entered international discourse in the aftermath of the Cold War and is thus perceived to be a post-colonial phenomenon largely affecting Sub Saharan Africa (Reno 1995). It was developed by a number of bodies and think tanks, including the Australian Strategic Planning Institute (ASPI) (Pha/Symon 2003), the Sydney Institute (Pha 2003), Zartman (2005), Ignatief (2004), and The Foreign Policy Centre. Mark Leonard of the Foreign Policy Centre refers to it as being a state where "the Cold War dichotomy of Freedom Versus Communism has been replaced with a new organizing principle: order versus disorder" (Leonard et al. 2002).

Implicit in the phrase, and the kind of philosophy of intervention being developed by the Foreign and Commonwealth Office and U.S. State Department, is a judgment on governments deemed to have failed to make the grade (Zartman/Kremeni 2005). A successful state, according to Zartman, is a stable, democratic, free-market country such as Britain or the United States. An unsuccessful state is believed to be one in which the government has brought failure on itself by dictatorial politics and outdated economics (Holsti 1995).

This work agrees with Ayoob's perspective on the matter, and contrasts with the one-sided Washington consensus (Ayoob 1999). The work questions if it is right that current instances of state failure are analysed in a historical vacuum and not seen as a part of the process of state making and state disintegration that have been integral components of the history of the modern system of states. State failure must be studied in proper historical perspective; current instances should be placed in the historical context of state building; and state collapse should be traced back to the formation of the earliest modern states in Europe.

Linking the analysis of state failure to the process of state making also emphasizes that instances of state failure are not unique to the present epoch but an inevitable part of the process of state making. Ayoob argues that "[a]nyone familiar with the history of modern Europe will immediately recall names like Aragon, Bohemia, Bavaria and Saxony as identifying putative political communities that were consigned to the dustbin of history because they failed to complete the process of sovereign state consolidation". They were unable to do so either because of internal vulnerabilities and weaknesses or because their sovereign existence did not suit the interests of major European powers for reasons related to the European balance of power or the processes of state building involving the major powers themselves.

In this context it is valuable to point out that there was no dearth of 'Sierra Leones' and 'Liberias' in 17th and 18th century Europe. Moreover, as Joseph Strayer (1973) points out, even for those that succeeded, "[i]t took four to five centuries for European states to overcome their weaknesses, to remedy their administrative deficiencies, and to bring lukewarm loyalty up to the white heat of nationalism".

1.2.   DEFINITION AND CLARIFICATION

It is important to define 'state failure' in a clear and workable way. In this research, a number of key terms are used: Thus, it is important to have a clear understanding of their meaning as they carry important connotations with them.

1.3.   DEFINITION OF STATE

A state - as defined by international law - should possess the following qualifications: (a) a permanent population; (b) a defined territory; (c) a government; and (d) the capacity to enter into relations with other states (Tilly 1990). Given the multiple definitions of the subject-matter within the realms of Social Sciences, this work is limited to Charles Tilly's classic definition of a state. According to Tilly, the contemporary state has, since its amorphous beginning a thousand years ago, acquired five salient characteristics which can be summarised as follows:

1. A territorially defined population with a paramount organ of government.

2. These organs are in turn served by specialized personnel - the civil service, which carries out decisions, and the military to back these.

3. The recognition of the state in its own defined territory as an independent state is also required by other states for its legitimacy. In fact it is this legitimacy that Tilly refers to as "sovereignty".

4. A community of feeling, a *Gemeinschaft* based on self-consciousness of a common nationality.

5. In practice, the population is formed into a community by the members, mutually sharing duties and benefits (Tilly/Ardant 1975).

By virtue of the above characteristics the concept of the state in international law is an entity with a fixed geographical boundary, a sizable and permanent population and a government with institutions that has firm control over security issues. Alden and Mbaya (2001) describe the state as the overall totality of elements, defined by traditional international law as population, territory and political organization. Clapham (2003) quotes Northedge's definition of State as a territory of people reorganized for the purposes of law and diplomacy as a legally equal member of the system of states. The United Nations Charter stresses the principles of sovereignty, independence and equal rights as the basic rights of all nations.

In England and in France, where the concept was largely developed, only the first three of Tilly's characteristics were visible during the medieval period, with the last two slowly acquired and becoming recognizable in the contemporary period. The last two characteristics are associated with nation-building whilst the first three with state-building. Both nation-building and state-building are characteristics embedded in a state. Tilly also stresses that a nation is an association living under common laws and represented by the same legislative assembly. A condition for being a nation, according to the above definition, is simply having "[p]opulations which have been consolidated under [a] common organ of government" (Tilly 1992). The United Nations Charter echoes the same by stressing that the following principles are important for the establishment of statehood: the principle of sovereignty; independence; equal rights as the basic rights of all nations; recognition of the state's claim to independence by other states; and enabling it to enter into agreements, although some omit the latter as a requirement - for instance, the Montevideo Convention.

1.4.   DEFINITION OF FAILED STATE

From the above discussion on the definition of a state as failed state can, therefore, be described as a state which does not meet all the criteria listed above on statehood: (1) a permanent population; (2) a defined territory; (3) a government; (4) the capacity to enter into relations with other states and the ability to exercise it; and (5) the monopoly of the use of force (Tilly 2000). Whether an entity is supposed to meet all the criteria before it is accepted as a state by the international community is another issue. Clapham (1996) argues that no state meets all the above criteria, not even the United Kingdom which is a model state. He argues that in 1997 the United Kingdom lacked firm control over Northern Ireland and parts of Scotland. However, it is clear that the degree of control over the citizens, the territory and the economic resources of a State are crucial to its existence.

A critical look at Brownlie's definition (1998) also supports the view that a state fails when it lacks state autonomy in the sense that there is no proper degree of freedom to manoeuvre for the state. For example, the long rule of Mobutu in Zaire is a typical reference. Domestically, there were no social groups that were sufficiently strong to challenge his position – he captured the state. The lack of adequate state capacity and statecraft characterised Mobutu's regime: lack of state capacity is defined as the absence of an efficient bureaucratic machinery guided and shielded by a political elite that gives priority to development; and lack of statecraft is the lack of the ability to formulate proper policy responses to given developmental challenges. It is based on this view that Zartman (1995) describes state failure as follows: "As the decision-making centre of government that is paralyzed and inoperative; laws are not made, order is not preserved, and societal cohesion is not enhanced ... As a territory, it is no longer assured security by a central sovereign organization. As the authoritative political institution, it has lost its legitimacy and as a system of socioeconomic organization, its functional balance of inputs and outputs is destroyed" (Zartman 1995: 5).

It is also widely accepted that the lack of a coherent national economy and capability of sustaining a basic level of welfare for the population of a state are indicators of the fragility of a nation. Although the poorest, least developed countries are in Sub-Saharan Africa, there are also considerable pockets of poverty in Central America and Asia (Burma, Nepal, and Bhutan). India, a country of enormous internal economic variation, has a relatively large part of the world's poor. Another determinant of fragile states is the political fabric of a nation. This refers to the institutions of the states and their legitimacy in the population. States that function well sustain a number of activities which are more or less taken for granted by their citizens: security against external and internal threats; order and justice in the sense of a functioning rule of law; and personal freedom including basic civil and political rights. However, fragile states sustain these functions only to a limited extent or not at all. In this respect, the institutions of the state are said to be weak, lacking capacity, competence, and resources. On the other hand, power is frequently concentrated in the hands of state elites who exploit their positions for personal gain. This is known in Sub-Saharan Africa as 'personal rule' or 'the strongman' (Jackson/Rosberg 1982).

According to Jackson and Rosberg (1982): "a state is said to have failed if it does not fulfil the most basic obligations of statehood". The leadership does not have the means and credibility to compel internal order, to deter or repel external aggression, and is unable to contain political or social fragmentation of its territory (Dearth 1996: 123). William Zartman, using the term 'state collapse', supports this view on state failure. According to him, state failure is "a situation where the structure, authority (legitimate power), law and political order have fallen apart and must be reconstituted in some form, old or new" (Zartman 1995: 1). Sorensen prefers the more general term 'fragile state' to denote a broader class of state with weakened economic and political institutions and processes, and reserves the term of state failure for cases "when fragility intensifies". Failed states may be described as states that are internationally recognised as sovereign territories, but which are nevertheless incapable of providing the domestic conditions of peace and good government discussed above.

No matter what definition one prefers, the essential characteristic that qualifies a 'failed state' is consistent and includes the following: a fundamental flaw in state institutions and government, and an increase in armed violence. If legislatures exist at all, they exist to ratify the decisions of a strong executive.

1.5.   DISTINCTION OF FAILURES

States can be classified as 'strong', 'weak', 'failed' or 'collapsed' states. The first is typified by its stronghold on the economy and in the exercise of a monopoly of the use of force as in the UK; the second can be described on the premise of the former Yugoslav State situation. The third encompasses a further erosion of legitimacy, while the fourth means the total collapse of state functions and capacity to govern. To understand what a failed state is as distinct from a successful one, it is important to understand what characterises a successful or a strong state. At its core, a successful state provides for the basic security of its population, protecting it from both internal and external threats. It also has the capacity to provide for the health and welfare of its population. Some states may never achieve the status of 'strong' and while they might not 'collapse', they may linger between a continuum ranging from weak to failed and from failed to collapsed. Somalia, Congo, Liberia, Sierra Leone and Bosnia are examples of states that have travelled on this continuum (Baker/Ausink 1996: 19-31).

According to Rotberg (2003), failed states provide only very limited quantities of essential political goods. A failed state is a hollow polity that is no longer willing or able to perform the fundamental tasks of a nation-state in the modern world. Its institutions are flawed. If legislatures exist at all, they ratify the decisions of a strong executive. Democratic debate is absent. The judiciary is derivative of the executive rather than being independent. Collapsed states, on the other hand, are rare and extreme versions of a failed state. They exhibit a vacuum of authority. They are mere geographical expressions, black holes into which failed policies have fallen.

Sub-state actors take over, and parts of the collapsed state may still exist and function but in an unrecognized and disordered manner. Collapsed states can only return to being failed, and then perhaps to being weak, if sufficient security is restored to rebuild the institutions and strengthen the legitimacy of the resuscitated state. Weak states can quickly become failed states, as the case of Cote d'Ivoire in 2002 demonstrates. In the aftermath of President Felix Houphouet-Boigny's death in 1993, his successors sought electoral success by appealing to Southerners due to being in the majority. They progressively began to discriminate against Northerners. Consequently, the expectations of rough equity that had long held the country together vanished. The legitimacy of the regime in charge vanished and Cote d'Ivoire, despite its decades of prosperity and success, and despite its ability to deliver many political goods, became ripe for failure (Kaplan 1996).

It follows that not all economically wanting states are necessarily weak in political-institutional terms. For instance, although Uruguay, Chile or Costa Rica are, in economic terms, referred to as Less Developed Countries (LDCs), this does not make them weak states. The reverse also holds – that is, not all states that are weak in political-institutional terms are LDCs. The Yugoslavia of yesterday and today's Bosnia, as well as Russia, could be classified as weak without being LDCs. Yet in most cases there will be an overlap, so that states which are politically-institutionally weak are also LDCs. It is in these states that the danger of becoming 'failed states' is most likely. While some of the least developed Central American states, the Central Asian states emerging out of the former Soviet Union, and some European states such as Albania share many of the characteristics of fragile states outlined above, Sub-Saharan Africa is unarguably home to most of the fragile states.

Table 1. Matrix on indicators used to define failed, weak, strong and collapsed states (Carment 2003).

Indicators	Strong	Weak	Failed	Collapse
Internal or External Security	High security	Basic level of security	No institution is responsible for security	Free for all (anarchy)
Extraction of Financial Resources	High level of tax collection	No efficient system of tax collection	No system of tax collection in place	Looting and banditry by warlords
Domestic Authority	High compliance with state institutions and the delivery of welfare	State institutions are in place but poorly performing	Absence of state institutions in most of the territory	Absence of state institutions and emergence of ethnic warlords

1.6.   RETHINKING SUB-SAHARAN STATEHOOD

To fully understand the debate and policy issues regarding failed state and post-war reconstruction within the international community, specifically as conducted by the Department for International Development (DfID), it is important that one first and foremost revisits colonisation and the reasons for withholding independence from these states in the first place. The problem with independence (Perham 1961: 26) is that most colonial territories at the time of independence, including Sierra Leone, lacked nearly all the attributes of coherent and viable communities, the most important being the absence of an idea of community - civic, natural, or otherwise. Yet they were granted independence because of the overwhelming support for it. Colonial societies are typically "politically weak, economically immature, socially divided, and their populations ignorant of the obligation of citizenship and unfamiliar with the working of modern government" (Bain 2001).

The eventual collapse of these states in the 1980s proved to a large extent the points of the critics who argued that only 'civilised' nations are entitled to membership in the international community. 'Barbarians', who know nothing but passion and violence, were thought to be incapable of respecting the laws of nations. It is for this reason that John Stuart Mill asserts that barbarians are not entitled to the right of nations: For they are fit only to be conquered and to be subject to foreign rule (Mill 1973: 377-78). John Lorimer similarly argues that barbarians and savage societies, inasmuch as they are unable to perform the duties of statehood, are entitled only to partial human recognition because they cannot be trusted to perform the duties of civilised nations. These societies, he argues, are populated by childlike races, and the right of undeveloped races, like the right of undeveloped individuals, is a right not to recognition as what they are not, but to guardianship - that is, to guidance - in becoming that of which they are capable in realising their special ideals.

As such, the granting of independence did not address an estimate of ability. For independence to mean anything, for it to contribute something valuable, it must be subjected to a test of competence. To proceed any other way would be to embark upon an uncertain journey fraught with danger. This was the path, Reno argues, Sierra Leone was said to have taken, and thus made its eventual collapse an inevitable one.

Is the case as simple and straight forward as Lorimer puts it? Today there are many explanations put forward by African academics challenging this hypothesis and giving evidence as to why African states find themselves disintegrated or failed as it is widely believed. The nature of African states is the first to be mentioned. As Kwabo (2008) posits, some states were born weak, as artificial constructs hewn out of colonial empires in Africa and Asia, a hybrid of the Westphalia state system imposed by their former occupiers (Amin/McDonagh 1973). It is a common factor that the Berlin conference of 1884/5 in partitioning Africa did not take into account the needs and wishes of ethnic groups. There is a saying in Ghana that a household in the north of Ghana has a part in Burkina Faso and part in Togo. This connotes the confusion caused by the forced demarcation of African territories. This implies that many ethnic groups were lumped together in one geographical entity without any commitment to nationhood (Nkrumah 1965). For example, Liberians have always grumbled that part of their land is in Sierra Leone (Clapham 1976). The Ewes in Ghana wish that they were with their kinsmen in Southern Togo (Herbst 2000).

The civil war in 1969-1970 in Nigeria over Biafra is also worth mentioning. It is as a result of this that most of the writers on failed states argue that one of the main causes of such phenomena is rooted in the lack of a common identity within the nation state (Clapham 1996). Pre-colonial states in Africa were 'non-hegemonic'. They were not meant to be the all powerful entities, monopolising politics and commanding societies that the colonial government was making them to be. This construct survived for centuries, even though they did not have the permanent precisely delineated boundaries described by the Weberian definition of a state. In pre-colonial Africa, power would dissipate the further a village was from the capital and would ebb and flow according to the fortunes of the central administration. This was very different from the European states of the time, where a government sought to be the sole source of political authority within rigidly defined territories.

1.6.1.   PATRIMONIAL STATEHOOD

Based on the above, it is not surprising that some commentators, including Reno, have argued that if Sierra Leone was a state, that state must have been a patrimonial one and not the legal bureaucratic state Weber seeks to describe (Reno 1995). Patrimonialism is a type of traditional rule or a political system that is dominated by a sovereign ruler (or a house of rulers) where both the army and the administration are dependent on the ruler. In Africa, this system was said to have been developed by the colonial government through its system of divide and rule. Reno's book, which provides a comprehensive explanation of the *modus operandi* of Sub-Saharan African political systems, argues that post-independent African rulers have, in taking over power from the colonial government, inherited the colonial patronage system and its lingering effect.

Reno then goes further to argue that the new post-Cold War environment has forced weak-state rulers to revise their political calculus. The work, which targets researchers, foreign business partners and policy makers, observes that political players on an affected ground often dismantle old patronage networks and form new alliances with compliant, often buccaneering foreign firms, bloating bureaucracies and privatised public-sector companies. In the aftermath, these firms become surrogate providers of bureaucratic services (especially security) in the enclaves where diamonds, cobalt, timber, or other valuable resources are extracted.

When this is not checked it eventually leads to sultanism, a hybrid form which combines both legal and patrimonial state systems. This hybrid form, 'neo-Patrimonialism' is characterised by combining patrimonial logic with a formal state bureaucratic system, or as Weber puts it, "from a structural point of view, the state is differentiated, but from a functional perspective it is weakly so; bureaucratic and patrimonial norms co-exist" (Weber 1968; transl. Roth/Wittich).

As a consequence of this, the most important positions in the state apparatus, whether in the bureaucracy, military, police or the national political frame, become filled with the loyal supporters of the strongman. Loyalty is strengthened through the (unequal) sharing of the spoils of office. The strongman controls a complex network of patron-client relationships. The functions of such a state have little to do with producing public or collective goods. The state apparatus becomes a source of income for those fortunate or clever enough to control it. Such a state is by no means a source of security, order, and justice for its citizens; it is more of a threat, an apparatus from which the population must seek protection. Against this background there is lack of legitimacy. Unfortunately, vertical legitimacy is low because large parts of the population have no reason to support such a government; and the government has no authority in the sense that people support or follow its rules and regulations. The people's sense of belonging together in the nation becomes weak simply because the state is captured by specific groups: it is no longer a state for all people. Christopher Clapham emphasises that such systems comprehensively lack "the capacity to create any sense of moral community amongst those who participate in them, let alone among those who are excluded" (Clapham 1996: 59).

1.7. FACTORS ASSOCIATED WITH STATE FAILURE

To avoid ambiguity, the factors of state failure will be considered in three distinct sets of empirical puzzles: The first associates state failure with macro level, long-term processes associated with system-wide transformations; the second emphasises intermediate perspectives; and the third emphasises micro-level strategic interactions between groups at specific points in time.

1.7.1. MACRO-LEVEL PERSPECTIVE OF STATE FAILURE

According to Norton and Miskel (1997), "changes in system structure can reverse state-building in several non-mutually exclusive ways: through the creation of highly dependent weak states (and the subsequent withdrawal of powerful patron-states) on the one hand and through processes of globalization and the strengthening of international norms of self-determination on the other". In Africa, there have been three such changes, the first with the slave trade, the second in colonisation and the third the Cold War. Most of these systemic transitions were associated with either the break up or the abrupt creation of new states in hostile environments, involving conflicts over territory and identity The post-Cold War era has, for instance, seen the disintegration of Yugoslavia and the collapse of Somalia, Liberia and Afghanistan. Another factor that fuelled these instabilities was superpower rivalry, which culminated in proxy wars and the influx of weapons into these states.

In advancing this argument of systemic changes, Holm argues that the new waves of weak states are "a function of how the international system developed and as a result failed when unfavourable systemic circumstances prevailed" (Holm 1998). Ayoob (1996) also supports this view by stressing that during the Cold War, weak states and the international community propped up corrupt leaders economically and militarily. This ensured that most of these states survived. But with the end of the Cold War, most of these states were left to sink or swim. Drawing from the above premise, failure can, therefore, be said to be a function of the withdrawal of outside support to weak states.

These changes brought by the Cold War (Herbst 2000), including the delivery of huge arms to new post-colonial states during the Cold War, operated as an independent factor for state collapse. Here the claim is made that, when the social compact between the governed and those governing breaks down, the availability of these arms leads quickly to the arming of contestants for the leading of state power. The provision of "small arms and light weapons" during the Cold War and after has continued to be a major slice of international assistance and global trade. Alger and Balasz comment that "conspicuously absent from the array of new threats to individual, national, and international security is a major weapons category that our leaders rarely mentioned" (Alger/Balasz 1985). The concluding observation is that such weapons are deadly, and when they are in the hands of even a relatively small group of persons they can provoke major state-threatening conflicts, in time leading to state collapse (ibid).

Even though some of the civil wars have roots in ethnic, religious, linguistic or communal enmity, the causes for these, as discussed above, can be traced as far back as the Congress of Berlin of 1884/85 with its forceful breakdown of communities, amalgamation of distant and inhospitable territories and the imposition of certain communities in a position of strength, both politically and economically. The resulting fear of the 'other' (and the consequent security dilemma) has driven much ethnic conflict and hostilities between regimes and subordinate and less favoured groups. Consistent with this view, Zartman (2004) notes that state collapse is marked by the loss of control not only of political but of economic space as well.

The discourse has been supported by a host of commentators. Alao et al. provide empirical evidence by arguing that most states fail due to the way they were formed: "colonialism brought people of different ethnic, political and religious affiliations together to form a state and forge a common sense of citizenship" (Alao et al 1999: 83-102). In addition, most African economies were incorporated into the European capitalist framework which made most of these economies structurally too weak to cope with the challenges of nation-building. In a similar vein, Herbst suggests that the 'paradox of decolonisation' in Africa stems from the formal colonization of Africa and the replacement of the continent's diverse political systems with an artificial state system which was carried forward in post-independent Africa (Herbst 1996: 97).

This supports the earlier hypothesis that there may not have been a state in Africa in the European sense of the word and thus, the term 'failed state' is by and large premature. How can a state fail when it has not even emerged? The vision that the new post-colonial African states were to build legitimate nations, provide wealth and guarantee security and perform all the tasks of a nation state within the span of a decade of achieving independence, as Chong (2003) notes, "was somewhat naïve". One can only expect such success from these newly independent states if the idea of State is taken completely out of historical context, and regarded as an entity that owes little or nothing to the forces that created it. However, another and maybe the right way to think about the contemporary anguish over state collapse is to note that what has collapsed is more the vision (or dream) (ibid: 10).

Jackson (1990) also enters this debate by noting that while some states in Asia defied the odds and succeeded in achieving the desired effect of the West, in Africa it resulted to the formation of what he called 'Quasi States'. These states, he argues, were never really states, and thus the puzzle is not how and why they may fail, but why they exist or persist at all. The idea that statehood is an appropriate institution in any environment is now being questioned and thus considered as an important impediment to the development to the African state. Therefore, it can be argued that the conflicts in Africa are a direct result of that act of commission or omission on the part of colonial governments. Alger and Balasz (1985) go even further, blaming the collapse on the colonial states: "the main problem was that most Western states failed to foresee that the self-determination of the 1960s was most certainly going to be followed by collapse". As a consequence, rather than blaming post-colonial leaders for the failure, one can argue that the emergence of modern authoritarianism in Africa stemmed from a series of interrelated phenomena that arose out of the colonial legacy and as a result was partly responsible for Africa's eventual collapse. For instance, whilst the availability of small arms and light weapons may operate as precipitating factors in the emergence of failed states, there is an element of uncertainty in that supplies of such weapons do not automatically or necessarily produce conflicts that lead to state collapse. The breakdown of the 'social contract' between the governed and those governing could be one of the underlying factors.

A nation state is said to fail when it loses legitimacy, when it cannot defend its nominal borders or when those borders become irrelevant. Once the state acquires the capacity to secure itself or to perform its duty in an expected manner, and once what little capacity remains is devoted almost exclusively to the fortunes of a few or to a favoured ethnic group or community, then there is every reason to expect less and less loyalty to the state on the part of the excluded and the disenfranchised. Baker and Ausink (1996) therefore see a collapsing state as one that has lost its legitimacy, has few functioning institutions, offers little or no public service to its citizens and is unable to contain fragmentation. This is much more relevant in Africa where most of the states that are plagued by state failure exist and where exclusive groups or classes have more ownership and control. As such, it is expected that the social contract, which binds inhabitants to an overarching polity, will become breached.

With the social contract between the state and the people breached, people stop trusting the state and, as occurred in Sierra Leone, they become sectional. Community security therefore becomes their main recourse in times of insecurity and their main source of economic opportunity. There is a tendency for people to transfer their allegiance to clan and group leaders who then become warlords able to derive support from external sources. In the wilder, more marginalised corners of failed states, terror can breed along with the prevailing anarchy that naturally accompanies state breakdown and collapse. This explains why the number of rebels in a particular country increases within a short period of time and the dynamics of African wars are swift. Thus in Sierra Leone rebel groups decided to use "the interests of the marginalised" to foster their interest (Abdullah 2004).

Carment and Harvey (2000) consider that this process has both internal and external implications. Hewitt (1997) supports this point by arguing that, "high levels of domestic instability limit a state's ability to act authoritatively within the international community, limit its ability to act on domestic society with any legitimacy, and to deliver socio-economic packages aimed at bringing about widespread industrialization" (ibid). Wallensteen (2005) sees the convergence of the internal and external dynamics as the ultimate basis for evaluating state performance. There are instances of decay where the state is under-consolidated – a situation where the state is not effective in the performance of its duties; and cases where the state is over-extended – and thus becomes a threat to its inhabitants (Richards 1996).

The economic failure of African States also accounts for their weakness. Most African states cannot feed their own people. Some people, especially government officials, manipulate government funds to their advantage. Rebel groups emerge to share in this booty. The international community usually intervenes in the form of economic aid, which usually comes with suicidal terms. Any state that goes about begging for food is a 'weak' or 'failed' state as it cannot take decisions on its own. The implementation of the Structural Adjustment Programme by the International Monetary Fund and its consequences on the economies of many African states attests to this claim. A good economy ensures political autonomy and without it a country cannot claim sovereignty. Further, whilst most African States can claim economic sovereignty, the majority of them have had their economies penetrated by multinational companies.

Their domestic politics are left in the hands of a few men who see themselves as elected to rule their people forever. The rise to power of Idi Amin in Uganda and Bokassa in the Central African Republic attest to this. Cruelty, financial mismanagement and corruption by these leaders led to the death of many in their countries. Some heads of states were even richer than the countries they governed.

1.7.2.   INTERMEDIATE AND MICRO-LEVEL PERSPECTIVES OF STATE FAILURE

The intermediate perspective is useful for understanding the root causes and background conditions leading to state failure (Buzan 1991) in identifying structural factors associated with decay and in accounting for changes in political, social and economic demands. They may, under some circumstances, also be able to explain why each side ends up fighting. But these factors cannot explain violent conflict. For instance, how long could a group of people tolerate denial of their ontological needs? Why do very similar countries, sharing the same cultural features most commonly associated with conflict and poverty, have different outcomes of state ability to govern? It can be said that salient ethnic or social divisions, minority grievances, failing government institutions and a lack of national identity produce radically different conflict histories. For instance, why does violence erupt in Zimbabwe and not in neighbouring Zambia? And why was there a Rwandan genocide in 1994 and not in 1990 when the Rwanda Patriotic Army (RPA) first invaded from Uganda? Why and how do states slip from weakness towards failure? What does it take to drive a failing state over the edge of collapse? The list goes on and on (Jackson 1982: 3).

Micro–level perspectives, therefore, seek to bridge this gap in our understanding by analysing it from three forms of dynamic interactions. The first are interactions between the belligerents themselves; the second, between the belligerents and outside forces who are in a position, through actions and statements, to alter the course of violence (Carment and Harvey 2001); and finally the role that avarice plays in propelling conflict. None of these indicators single-handedly provides evidence that a strong state is becoming weak or a weak state is heading pell-mell into failure. But a judicious assessment of all three and other factors discussed in this chapter, taken together, should provide both quantitative and qualitative warnings.

1.7.3.   GROUP AND SOCIETY REACTION

The first dynamic, between the belligerents, escalates to violence in situations where governing elites, driven by ethnic or other communal hostility, or by insecurities, victimize their own citizens or some sub-sets of the community. An example is the case with Mobutu, where ruling cadres increasingly oppressed, extorted and harassed the majority of their own compatriots while privileging a narrowly based party, clan, or sect. In such a state of broken social contracts, the environment becomes conducive for ethnic or conflict entrepreneurs to mobilize support.

As such, the level of violence resulting from the denial of needs then accounts for the second indicator of state failure (Azar 1986). Burton's (1990b) human needs theory also supports this view. In "Human Theory of Conflict", J. W. Burton postulates that in addition to the obvious biological needs of food and shelter, there are basic socio-psychological human needs such as identity, security, recognition, participation and autonomy which relate to growth and development. In his view, such development needs must be catered for if societies are to remain significantly free of conflicts. This is because whereas an individual is responsive to opportunities for the improvement of his/her life style, he/she refuses to accept the denial of ontological needs like security, dignity etc. As a result, any political system that denies or suppresses these human needs eventually generates protest and conflict (Burton 1990b). This issue will be discussed in detail in Chapter 2.

However, do the steady erosion of the economy and the increasing inability of people to meet their basic needs lead to the collapse of legitimate governance? Or does the collapse of legitimate governance lead to the steady erosion of the economy? For the purpose of this thesis, it is not necessary to answer such questions. What is important, however, and what has become increasingly clear is that economic collapse presents cases of state failure. In such cases, however costly and irrational it appears in human and material terms, violence becomes an important aspect in ensuring group solidarity, regulating behaviours and maintaining social hierarchy. In short, a collective group will pursue violence if it safeguards advantageous and long-term political and economic outcomes for them (ibid). This is little more than a Maslovian argument but it seems to be lost in much of the debates and policy documents as to why states fail and most importantly, how to reconstruct them. In my view, this economic dimension of the problem is essential for constructing a strategy for responding to state failure or basically the path out of state failure must be paved with economic development and economic stability.

1.8.   DEMOCRACY

Democracy is predominantly a new phenomenon which the UN and most international institutions have ascribed to, to address today's peace-building crisis - the rationale for it is that democracy addresses the economic, social, cultural, humanitarian and political roots of conflicts. It constitutes a comprehensive method of approach covering the broad range of new peace-building priorities: 'top-down' international regulation of elections, institutional development and economic management; and also 'bottom-up' assistance to develop a democratic political culture through civil society building (Chandler 1999: 110).

The result derived from these approaches has provided the international community the opportunity to respond to current and prevailing post-conflict issues, which have also become a challenge to them and a dilemma to war-affected nations. Like democracy, the term peace-building was also of late introduced into the efforts of the international community in their current strive to upgrade the response of both governmental and non-governmental organizations (NGOs) to armed conflicts and its devastating consequences. In its broad term, peace-building is also noted as a "reflection on new resolve to search for ways of responding earlier, more consistently, and less chaotically to conflicts" (Ploughshares 1995: 1).

However, despite a decade of the international community's involvement in war zones, commentators are inclined to believe that the United Nations, regional organizations, national governments and NGOs still remain ill-prepared in terms of building lasting peace in regions of current or potential conflicts. The complications normally encountered when it comes to deal with conflict resolution in regions prone to insurgence or recurrence of fights and the like, still continue unabated. The international community is consequently faced with series of failures. This, in most cases, causes the international community to shift much attention to prescribing a democratic culture which is expected to consolidate a culture of peace. The challenges in the political arena and the structured scheme of approach have made democracy, as seen by political actors and the populace, as "the right and natural order of things" (Sorenson 1998: 102).

Regarding peace-culture that democracy is expected to exhibit, this part of the work takes a brief look at already concluded peace-building efforts to examine whether democracy precluding peace-building has been successful in exhibiting pacifying effects. The context or situations where such peace-building efforts have been employed are very essential. In view of the claim that democracy yields a counterpoising effect when implemented under incompatible circumstances, this subchapter examines the dominant ideas that have been shaping the approaches by international institutions and arguments for and against those approaches in implementing its blueprint within the framework of democratization.

1.8.1. DEMOCRATIZATION

Schumpeter sees democracy as an "institutional arrangement for arriving at political decision in which individuals acquire the power to decide by means of competitive struggle for people's vote" (Schumpeter 1943: 269). This has been included in the efforts of international institutions in post-conflict settings, which have stimulated interesting debates. One of the earlier arguments is from Immanuel Kant in his essay "Perpetual Peace" (1795): Kant stated that it is a natural tendency for states to form a liberal democratic view point since democracy bestows legitimacy on the rulers which makes them capable of facing international threats. In other words, "states not organized as liberal republics will tend to be unsuccessful" (Sorenson 1999: 93), while states with a democratic culture will, through the pacifying effect of democracy, lead to a stable peace due to the fact that democracies rule through the people's consent. In Kant's words, "if the consent of citizens is required in order to decide that war should be declared…nothing is more natural than that would be very cautious in commencing such a poor game, decreeing for themselves all the calamities of war. Among the latter would be: having to fight, having to pay the cost of war from their own resources, having painfully to repair the devastation war leaves behind, and, to fill up the measures of evils, load themselves with heavy national debt that would embitter peace itself and that can never be liquidated on account of constant wars in the future" (Kant 1983: 100). In sum, Kant's argument in support of that democratization leads to peace derived from his claim that the mere existence of democracies, with its culture of peaceful conflict resolution; the bond or common moral values that democracies share which he refers to as a pacific union; the economic cooperation between democracies, which when added together he believed will act as a recipe for peace to flourish between democracies; and with its spread will then affect the whole world.

This view have also been shared and supported by Joseph Schumpeter and R. J. Rummel, who according to his empirical research into Libertarian States, stated that in conflicts in the period 1976-1980, only 24 percent of free states (meaning those that emphasize political and economic freedom) (Sorenson 1999: 94) were involved in comparison to 26 percent of partly free and 61 percent of the non-free states. His conclusion states that "the more libertarian a state is, the less it is involved in foreign violence" (Rummel 1983: 27-71). In other words, democratic states are more peaceful than non-democratic ones.

Social scientists and commentators have for years supported Kant's views on democracy. With their findings, Schumpeter and Rummel have both brought new impetus to the optimistic view. And of late the former UN Secretary General Boutros Boutros-Ghali in his report entitled, "An Agenda for Peace", he gave political currency to the concept of peace-building which calls for "western democratic principles, declaring that, periodic and genuine election are a crucial factor in the effective enjoyment of a wide range of other human rights" (United Nations 1992). It concludes with the assertion that "democracy is one of the pillars on which a more peaceful, more equitable, and more secured world can be built" (ibid).

Axworthy also reiterated this sentiment when in his speech at York University in the creation of a new Canadian peace-building mechanism expressed the same sentiment about bringing assurance to the optimistic view. However, Melvin Small and J. David Singer have questioned these hopes in their research: they came to conclude that there is no significant difference between democracies and other regimes and that democracies are as war-prone as other types of governments. Commentators and Realists have pursued this argument against democracy. Realism here refers to "a theoretical perspective on International Relations that purports to analyze the world as it really is, not as it ought to be" - the definition stated therefore supports the view that conflict is a fact of life and inevitable due to the forces inherent in human nature (Hoffman 1996: 160). It is very crucial here that the arguments made for democracy only emphasize that democracies do not fight each other in the international arena and not within themselves - as most African countries have in the contemporary period been experiencing intra-state wars.

Roland Paris is one of the most forceful commentators against democracy, who refers to the present approach of the international community as 'Liberal Internationalism'. He defined it, in its broadest sense, as an active involvement of international affairs, which is believed to be the opposite of isolationalism and internationalism. He also stated: "it connotes foreign policies that develop to enhance multilateral cooperation among states" (Paris 2001). The two concepts comprising liberal internationalism suggest an activist foreign policy that promotes liberal principles abroad, especially through multilateral cooperation and international institutions. To sum it up, Paris noted that as a single paradigm, liberal internationalism has been governing the conduct of peace-building in the post-Cold War era. It involves a regime change from beginning to the end, including both stages of what is generally termed, in comparative literature, as "transition" to a liberal democracy and its subsequent "consolidation" (Pridam and Vanhanen 1994: 2). However, as will be illustrated in the following chapters, a regime change does not always achieve the aim of peace-building.

1.8.2.   THE PARADOX OF DEMOCRATIZATION ON PEACE-BUILDING

One argument has been overlooked in the literature, that is, both democracy and capitalism encourage conflict and competition. Its also refers back to the definition of democracy by Schumpeter: democracy is an institutional arrangement for arriving at a political decision in which individuals acquire the power to decide by a means of a competitive struggle. Schumpeter noted that democracy thrives on competition and requires politically active and involving citizenry. Commentators refer to it as "a vibrant civil society" (Paris 2001) in order to counter-balance and scrutinize the power of the state and to provide a channel of expression. Indeed, democratic societies accept that conflict is a fact of life and seek to intensify it in areas where it is latent with the hope of channelling it through existing institutions (Fisher 1999). Coser, who first explored the stabilization effect of societal conflict, also explained this paradox: "by permitting the immediate and direct expression of rivalry claims; open societies are able to adjust their structures by eliminating the sources of dissatisfaction" (Coser 1956). However, amidst all these claims, Dahl noted that, "encouraging political activity can polarize the populace into a number of separated, potentially hostile communities" such as in Africa where multiparty democracy divides the populace along ethnic lines into separate ethnic cocoons. In view of this dilemma, Dahl went further to caution that "when a society is divided in this way, it may reinforce societal differences and work against the goal of establishing a stable democratic system particularly if ambitious politicians deliberately exploit inter-group differences to build a following" (Sandbrook 1996).

This problem is supposed to have escalated the conflicts in nearly all the eight United Nations peace-building programmes - beginning from Namibia, El Salvador, Mozambique up to Sierra Leone. He concurs with Georg Sorenson's assertion that to assume that "Democracies do not fight each other" as "one of the strongest nontrivial or non-tautological statement that can be made about international relation" (ibid), and as such democracy can be inherently violent like any others. This view has also been supported by commentators like Francois Furet (1985) who argued that "the adversarial politics of democracy can sharpen confrontations and conflict in divided societies, rather than fostering greater tolerance for different interests and opinions".

1.8.3.   EFFECTS OF ECONOMIC LIBERALIZATION POLICIES

Like democracy, capitalism also thrives on conflict and competition by which society competes for a large share of a country's economy - an approach which seems fair but when replicated in some post conflict situations, it can yield counter-intentional results. Therefore, it has rendered a lot of criticism from commentators for various reasons; for instance, it creates economic inequalities that have historically fuelled resentment and confrontation.   It exhibited detrimental effects through its structural adjustment programmes implemented through the IMF and World Bank. The programmes comprise structural changes and current management components: the former require countries to accept capitalist market forces, which compels governments to privatize. The latter further requires governments to accept so-called international standards. It also involves depreciating the exchange rate and decontrolling prices, reforming the tax system, reducing the fiscal deficits and maintaining tight controls on credit.

These policies promote economic liberalization as a recipe for stable economic growth in the long run. However, they often lead to economic hardship and political instability in the short run. Mozambique and El Salvador are examples where those policies have, instead of alleviating potential conflicts, rather exacerbated those through SAP. This then concurs with Fisher's definition of violence: "actions, words, attitudes, structure or systems that cause physical, psychological, social or environmental damage and/or prevent people from reaching their full human potential" (Fisher 1999). This definition does not limit violence to killing, beating, torture, maiming and so on. According to new definitions of violence, it also comprises equally damaging elements of violence such as killing with a gun, killing through deprivation of foods and other essential needs to sustain lives - a punishment believed to have been imposed by international institutions or one in which one group of nations imposes deliberate suffering on others.

War-shattered states that had to borrow large sums of money in order to rebuild their economies were faced with the consequential dilemma to be conditioned to restructure their economies in order to pay those debts. In most of the circumstances, it has caused severe hardship that have in return resulted in conflicts. It has been further complicated by the fact that leaders of the North and South are colluding into such arrangements whilst the rest of the people suffer. The result of such actions can be seen as "structural or institutional violence" (Fisher 1999).

All of these problems come at the expense of the international community's belief in the power of the ballot box, which it hopes can bring about peace and stability. Experience as well as empirical research have proven this notion to be naive and false since "the process of political and economic liberalization is inherently tumultuous and disruptive" (Paris 1997).

1.8.4   THE NEED FOR CRITICAL THINKING

What have we learned about democratization and liberalization, and how does it affect our understanding of peace-building? Boutros-Ghali's "Agenda for Peace" still informs our understanding of peace-building, rather than diminishing our faith in the efficacy of peace-building. It has been argued "democracy is an unaffordable luxury for most developing countries where the need for development will outweigh the need for accountable governments" (Ake 1967). With democracy under the barrel of the gun, commentators have come up with various alternatives, which I will briefly examine. Paris states that an authoritarian solution for war-shattered states should not be rejected out of hand but cautions at the same time of promoting authoritarianism as a peace-building strategy. However, this will raise serious problems in most circumstances. A democratic government is preferable since it encompasses the institutions through which conflicts can be resolved.

A second alternative is that of partition, which divides a war-shattered state into territorial discrete, political independent units. The resulting entities are to exist as sovereign states or autonomous regions within existing states. Chaim Kaufman endorsed this by noting that violent conflict hardens ethnic identities to the point that cross-ethnical political appeal becomes futile, meaning that victory can be assured by physically controlling the territory in dispute. However, he also noted some problems associated with this - the unwillingness of the international community to perform its task of providing the necessary security. A typical example of this is the Bosnian scenario, where the international community declared a safe area of Srebrenica and then stood by to allow it to be overrun in July 1995 by Bosnian Serbs, who then systematically killed thousands of civilians.

However, it is not to be assumed that by the mere setting up of a democratic government, especially in conflict zones, peace will result easily. And so it requires that before addressing any political and/or social conflict in war-shattered states, donor agencies and NGOs alike are to seek a better understanding of the cultures, dynamics, relationships and issues of the situation before drafting a method of approach - an approach, which pays no respect to any blueprint or democracy per-se but is specific to the conflict in question.

Such an approach might in some cases not be compatible with the political reforms as democratic programmes basically tend to focus on constructing enduring structures to succeeding generations rather than on an environment of basic order and stability with sustainable resources. Thus, depending on the given context and stability of the environment, a peace-building approach focusing on short-term measures might be more feasible in an early stage of peace-building until mid-term and long-term democracy-enhancing measures can be implemented.

1.9.   THE DUTY TO INTERVENE

In the face of violence, especially from non-state actors, it is the belief of the state that it is its right to exercise "the monopoly of the legitimate use of physical force within its territory to restore order" (Tilly et al. 1987). Tilly et al. go on to suggest that while the successful use of coercion by a state in order to suppress local ethnically-based challenges in some cases enhances the assessment of its future utility, coercion against minority ethnic groups without consent can also be a normative factor since elites who use violence become habituated to violence (ibid). While the state's use of force helped to define it, drawing from Weber's conclusion, Mason warns "when force is used, the authority itself has failed".

According to Hobbes (Schmitt 1996), "sovereignty is a combination of coercive power and consent, and it is this combination that provides legitimacy to political authority and resolves the problem of order within societies." The coercive power of the sovereign will alone never be sufficient to maintain a political order. Only if the people understand why the polity must be ordered, and only if they continue to view the sovereign as a legitimate authority and trust in its judgment, can a political order be secure. Therefore, state strength, when the state has failed, can only be achieved through negotiation with society rather than abrasion against it. Furthermore, legitimacy and state capacity are intimately related, and the state's primary and routine reliance on force, in order to have its commands obeyed, signifies a drastic reduction in its legitimacy. As Baker and Ausink (1996) have pointed out succinctly, "A state which can only coerce its subjects is not governing them; it is at war with them."

In Africa, foreign interventions have been both frequent and varied, with both constructive and negative consequences. On the one hand, while foreign intervention helps to salvage war torn societies; on the other hand, foreign intervention complicates nation building as was the case with Mozambique. The same can be said also of the Economic Community of West African States Cease-Fire Monitoring Group (ECOMOG), UNOMIL and UNAMSIL, in Liberia and Sierra Leone respectively. One thing to note here is that European intervention did not begin in the post-Cold War era of independent states. In fact, such intervention led to the colonial wars during the colonial scramble for Africa in the nineteenth century. Uhomoibhi observes that the Berlin conference, held at the behest of European powers in 1884-1885, during which African territories were partitioned, was international intervention par excellence.

Zartman (2004) pushes this debate regarding the motive of intervening parties further by examining some other reasons why it is carried out. In Africa, he believes that interventions have defined objectives. In some cases it is for protecting the life and property of its citizens, as was the case with France and Belgium in the Congo. In other cases, it is primarily to profit from the spoils of African states – what some critics have called "crass opportunism" (Mair 2008). Another objective was to foster a specific geographic and political interest, as was the case with the Cold War. To conclude on this section on foreign intervention, the evidence available suggests that foreign intervention did not necessarily provide a full or early solution to the perennial problem of state instability and state cohesion.

1.10.   GIVE WAR A CHANCE?

While war is evil, third party intervention does in rare circumstances help to exacerbate conflict when the conflict is not allowed to run its natural course: conflicts have typically been interrupted early on, before they could burn themselves out and establish the preconditions for a lasting settlement (Luttwak 2005). Luttwak goes further to controversially note that, "too many wars nowadays are becoming endemic conflicts that never end because the transformative effects of both decisive victory and exhaustion are blocked by outside intervention". In addition, if and when conflicts are left to run their course, he questions the policy of the USA, for example, to back one side with the hope that it emerges as the winner and that it can reorder the affairs of the country. This tack was tried repeatedly throughout the Cold War, often with poor results (ibid).

On the humanitarian assistance front, NGOs are said to have in many cases exacerbated the very conflicts and violence they were seeking to relieve by bringing in new resources into a conflict situation (Anderson 1999). During war, each side tries to acquire and control resources, and so NGO aid can present a new focus for struggle. Anderson lists a number of ways in which NGO assistance can become distorted and actually contributes to the conflict. Warring factions, she argues, may "tax the NGO for the right to deliver their aid" (ibid). Those 'taxes' then support the war effort. Aid may be stolen and redirected to the fighting parties. Resources given to victims may be passed on to friends and relatives who are engaged in fighting. NGO-built infrastructure, such as roads, may enable military troops to travel further and faster. Local, NGO-trained specialists may be conscripted into military service.

NGO actions and attitudes can also exacerbate conflict. Anderson (ibid: 48) notes, "NGOs must choose to employ some people (and not others), purchase goods from some (and not others), and target their aid toward some people (and not others); these decisions can fuel separate group identities, inequalities, and jealousies." Publicizing human rights abuses can provoke both increased outrage and a defensive response in the perpetrators, and so further harden their opposition. Such publicity can also promote a dehumanized image of the perpetrators. Accordingly outside forces can be mutually reinforcing, mutually exclusive, or mutually incompatible.

1.11. CONCLUSION

This chapter has sought to examine the concept of the failed state and, in particular, the historical, group and societal factors, both internal and external, that contribute to weak, collapsed and failed states, as the basis for subsequent analysis of the Sierra Leonean situation. Today, most of the debates on Africa in general and Sierra Leone in particular have mainly focused on definitional issues, the strengths and weaknesses of contending methodologies and evaluation procedures as well as the causes, manifestations and processes of state failure. Much less attention has been paid to the question of how Sierra Leone fits within the European notion of statehood and to what extent that link has contributed to state decay.

In the history of the world no country has developed without the State and its people playing a central and proactive role. This has to be taken into consideration if the African State is to be made more relevant towards the development of the continent. It can be inferred from Edward Said (2003) that Africans need to do more to keep the memories of the past and present alive, which would enable them to shape their destiny for a better future.

2

THEMATIC REFLECTION

THEMATIC REFLECTION ON WAR TO POST-WAR RECONSTRUCTION TRANSITIONS

2.1. INTRODUCTION

Intra-state conflicts are now far more common than international conflicts. Of the 25 major armed conflicts listed by the Stockholm International Peace Research Institute for 2000, all but two were internal (Collier et al. 2000). Ayoob (1996) estimates that in 1995 alone at least 14 Sub-Saharan countries with a total estimated population of 175,000,000 experienced intra-state conflicts and thus demanded the use of post-war reconstruction. It is interesting to note that apart from the successful Marshall Plan after World War II and aid to Uganda in the 1980s, most of the post-war reconstruction programmes - especially those directed towards countries coming out of civil war - have failed. This includes UNOSOM, Liberia and even Sierra Leone after 1997.

Robert Jackson (1990) believes that the primary reason for such failures rests in the conceptual deficit evident in official discourses in understanding the nature of these wars, and the theoretical vacuum in regard to their causes (Jackson 2002: 3). The net result is that many of the world's poorest countries are locked in a tragic and vicious circle where poverty causes conflict and conflict causes poverty. Eighty percent of the world's 20 poorest countries have suffered a major war in the past 15 years. On average, countries coming out of war face a 44 percent chance of relapsing in the first five years of peace (Goodhand/Hulme 1999). Why and how can this trend be reversed? And why post-war reconstruction and not nation building? This chapter addresses the theory and taxonomy of state failure. The following chapter will narrow it to Sierra Leone. It addresses the method of reversing state failure and the role of elections and socio-economic factors. The demobilising of combatants and civil society are among the many topics this chapter will discuss.

2.2.   THEMATIC UNDERPINNING OF THE STUDY

Theoretical understanding is necessary to provide a sound basis and sharper insight into any work of academic significance. It is for this reason that the following paradigms are examined:

- 'General Theory of Conflict' (the need to know what it is before attempting to resolve it);

- Theories on intervention (in conflict and post-war situations).

2.3.   HUMAN NEEDS THEORY

In the African context, it can be argued that ethnic heterogeneity per se is not the cause of conflict. Rather, it is policies and institutions that attempt to deny some ethnic groups security, identity, recognition, participation and autonomy. Hardly any one theory can adequately explain the sources of conflict and the failure that results, but the human needs theory as a framework of analysis of conflicts in Africa has a number of advantages. First, it rejects ethnicity and religious sentiments and focuses on structural and institutional deformities as the primary source of conflict. Secondly, it emphasizes that basic human needs are universal and that their frustration anywhere constitutes a threat to social peace and order. Thirdly, it holds that the satisfaction of basic needs is central to the functioning of political institutions. An application of this theory to the Sierra Leonean situation leads us to examine how the exclusionary policies of the colonial government and later how the All People's Congress era and the repressive Momoh regime contributed to the outbreak of the war and the eventual collapse of the Sierra Leonean state.

2.4. STUDY ON THE THEORY OF CONFLICT AND CONFLICT RESOLUTION

Coser (1956) defines conflict as "a struggle over values or claims to status, power and scarce resources in which the aims of the conflicting parties are not only to gain the desired value but also to neutralise, injure or eliminate their rivals". This definition intimates the types of values over which parties in conflict struggle. They could be tangible resources like food, money, land, mineral resources, etc., or intangible ones like power, status, identification, etc. But it is not always easy to draw the line – a particular conflict could be over a combination of these. In particular, the Sierra Leone crisis, which began with a struggle for power, became one of acquisition and exploitation of the country's natural resources.

Coser's definition also places emphasis on the destructive aspect of conflict – the opposing parties in their attempts to achieve their goals try to neutralise their competitors or even to destroy them. But Stedman (1991) is of the view that conflict does not necessarily lead to violence (or the destruction of the opponent). It is when peaceful mechanisms for pursuing competing interests fail that violence emerges. This supports Stedman's view that, "Although conflict may turn violent, violence is not an inherent aspect of conflict but rather a potential form that conflict may take" (ibid: 270). He cautions that, "concerns about security and survival co-exist with the issues that caused the conflict" (ibid: 388). Arguably, Stedman maintains that, given the circumstances in the above situation, resolution of conflict necessarily becomes more difficult since it must deal with the two levels – the underlying causes of the conflict and the ending of the violent expression of it.

Zartman (1995) emphasises that the potentially violent nature of conflict, therefore is a dilemma which governments face in dealing with demands and grievances before situations get out of hand and erupt into violence. Although he recommends that governments handle demands and grievances at an early stage, he observes that governments are often reluctant to do so. This explains why at the initial stages of the National Patriotic Front of Liberia (NPFL) incursion into Liberia, the Doe government tried to downplay its significance.

Goodman and Bogard (1992) consider that for a negotiation to succeed in reaching a settlement, there should be an element of doubt on both sides. In their view, "if one side of a military conflict remains convinced that they have the time and resources to achieve their original goals, then they may enter negotiations with a slate of concealed motive" (ibid: 52). Such motives could be to test the determination of the other side to continue to fight or to allow for time to regroup their forces and prepare for a new offensive. The attitude of the NPFL, which occupied most of Liberia for much of the time during the peace process, confirms the above assertion.

In their analysis of the conceptual bases of conflict resolution, Deng et al. (1996) highlight the fact that conflicts are usually approached from the perspective of the key leaders of the conflicting factions. While the role of such leaders cannot be ignored if any settlement is to succeed, it is essential to remember that often there exist differences between the objectives of the elites, the fighting men and the populace. Usually, the faction leaders are more concerned with the struggle for power and less for the lives of the ordinary citizens and the welfare of the community as a whole. The relevance of this point to the Liberian crisis was clearly demonstrated in 1994 when, after the Akosombo Accord ceded power on the Council of State to the faction leaders, the civilians demonstrated in protest and eventually institutionalised their protest in the formation of the Liberation National Conference of Unarmed Citizens. There were also instances where the leaders negotiated peace whilst their combatants continued fighting.

2.5.   STUDIES ON INTERNAL CONFLICTS

Brown (1996) identifies three causes of internal armed conflicts. These are bad leadership; a strong sense of antagonistic history; and mounting economic problems. While it may seem simplistic to attribute the causes of all internal conflicts to just three factors, one cannot deny that those three factors were crucial in the Sierra Leone case. Momoh's regime was one in which he did almost everything to perpetuate himself: the relationship between his Limba tribe and its Southern and Eastern neighbours the Mende was strained, and the economy was in far worse shape in 1992 than it was in 1985, when he took over.

Zartman (1995) takes the peculiar problems of resolving internal conflicts further. He contends that internal conflicts are most difficult to negotiate because of their asymmetrical structure in which one party is strong and the other is weak both in terms of military power and legitimacy. At the same time, he sees negotiations as a better option for resolving internal conflicts than military victory. This is because a defeat of the rebellion often only drives the cause underground to emerge at a later date while victory for the rebellion may "carry with it the mirror image of the previous exclusions, triggering new repressions and exclusions". The difficulty is that the intensity of internal conflicts prevents the parties from either communicating with each other or thinking of a mutually attractive solution.

In such circumstances, mediation by a third party becomes crucial. Yet mediation is difficult in a civil war, because the parties - for different reasons - are very reluctant to accept third party intervention. To the government side the mediator necessarily interferes in its domestic affairs and also recognizes and legitimises the rebellion. The rebels, on the other hand, are suspicious that the interveners would support the government and prevent the rebellion from running its course. The net effect is that internal conflicts tend to be protracted unnecessarily.

It is true that the case studies in Zartman's edited book, "Elusive Peace" do not include the Sierra Leonean crisis but his introductory discourse is generally applicable to the war dynamics and the settlement process in Sierra Leone. However, Zartman fails to consider the effects of other structural elements of internal conflicts, which mitigate against a negotiated settlement: He ignores structural obstacles such as the leadership conundrum and security dilemma and others, which King (1997) elucidates. This work takes a broader view and examines other obstacles to the peace process in Sierra Leone.

2.6. STUDIES ON STRUCTURAL OBSTACLES AND INTERVENTION STRATEGIES

Civil wars are known to prolong to the extent that belligerents tend to continue fighting even when it is apparent that doing so is no longer necessary (King 1997: 29). Traditionally, this phenomenon has been explained in terms of irrational acts of individual combatants or incompatible beliefs of the opposing sides (ibid: 56). King (1997) accepts that all civil wars contain elements of the two factors mentioned above, but introduces an additional theoretical explanation which he calls "structural elements of war fighting in internal conflicts" (ibid: 13). He further points out that uncovering the incentive for violent conflict (through the structural obstacle approach) reveals a better picture of the reasons for war from the perspective of the belligerents themselves. More significantly, it provides potential targets for outside mediators wishing to hasten the conclusion of a durable peace accord.

King identifies five main structural obstacles to resolving internal conflicts, namely leadership conundrum; diffuse decision-making and enforcement mechanisms; the gap between the military situation and political objectives; asymmetry in commitment, status and organization; and security dilemma. Each of them is briefly examined here to highlight its relevance to our study.

The problem with leadership arises partly because particular leaders may be so committed to the cause of the struggle or to retaining power that they are incapable of contemplating some form of compromise with the enemy. Some leaders (especially the insurgent group) may prefer fighting on and losing rather than returning to the *status quo ante*. Worse still, as the war drags on, combatants on either side come to identify their own leadership with the struggle itself and refuse to accept any negotiated settlement that would diminish the status of the leadership.

Problems of decision-making and enforcement arise in all conflicts because within the same group belligerents may be divided over the utility of continued war. The situation is particularly serious in civil wars because "[f]actionalism among warring elites is often extremely intense, with belligerent parties breaking apart and reforming, coalitions appearing and dissolving and erstwhile allies becoming sworn enemies" (King 1997: 34). In addition, the non-traditional nature of combatants in civil wars can inhibit the leaders' ability to communicate their desire to end hostilities to their subordinates. The culture of violence spawned by the war makes the combatants reluctant to surrender their weapons and return to civilian life. This is because apart from the gun guaranteeing their own safety, it also becomes their source of livelihood.

King argues that the assumption that parties normally accept the situation on the battlefield as a basis for peace does not apply in the case of civil war. For instance, the gulf which often exists between the situation on the battlefield and the negotiation table arises partly because civil wars by nature involve a relatively small space for compromise between the warring factions. The leaders in both camps see anything short of total elimination of the enemy as a form of defeat. For this reason, the military option remains foremost in their minds. More significantly, the original political objective that prompted the turn to violence may be lost as a result of interests developed in the course of the war. Belligerents may still pay lip service to their original political goals but the insurgent group may now have an interest in the continuation of violence that would ensure that funds raised from exploitation of resources remain solidly in rebel hands. Those original objectives may be transformed by the war experience itself.

The asymmetrical relationship, which exists between contesting parties in civil wars, is another disincentive to a negotiated settlement. Warring factions in civil wars have marked disparities in terms of commitment, status and organization. Whereas for the insurgent group, commitment to the insurgency is all consuming and a matter of life-and-death, for the incumbent group, countering the rebellion is only one of the issues it must attend to. Thus, the incumbent group has to balance its commitment to fighting the rebellion with other tasks of everyday governance. In terms of status, the incumbent party enjoys international recognition, a seat at the UN, membership of regional organizations and some degree of popular legitimacy but the insurgents have to fight for all these privileges. In addition, the incumbent perceives the insurgent group as illegitimate and refuses to recognize it as a bargaining partner while the latter challenges the legitimacy of the incumbent. Regarding organization, the incumbent group, at least initially, is better organized with professional soldiers, while the insurgent forces are composed of non-traditional combatants (including child soldiers), concerned more with their survival than long-term strategic operations (ibid: 54).

The conditions of widespread violence which civil wars spawn tend to create distrust between belligerent sides that is detrimental to negotiated settlement. Due to a high level of distrust between the warring factions, each of the opposing sides tends to reserve a residual fighting force as a deterrent should the other renege on a negotiated settlement. The dilemma is that the reserved forces present a security threat to the opposing side and this in turn justifies each side's unwillingness to disarm and accept a negotiated settlement.

Subsequent chapters of this study will reveal that King's paradigm of structural obstacles provides a very useful template to understanding why the Sierra Leone conflict lingered longer than DfID had initially anticipated. The second part of King's analysis concentrates on the extent to which third parties (such as individual states, external powers, or regional organizations) may help circumvent the structural obstacles and promote a durable negotiated settlement. King prescribes a number of strategies, which he himself admits are not foolproof but provide useful guidelines for third party intervention. A few of these strategies are illustrated in the following segments.

The first is to take advantage of leadership changes within the factions and to use the uncertain period after the departure of key leaders to press ahead with negotiations. While the mediators may benefit from the willingness of the new leadership to reassess the utility of continued conflict, there is also the possibility that a new leader might disassociate himself from the former's commitment to negotiate.

The second strategy is insistence on the removal of recalcitrant leaders as a prerequisite for negotiation or as a component of a final peace settlement (ibid: 63). This prescription, however, looks more problematic than beneficial. It may easily boomerang and derail the peace process. Labelling a particular leader as an obstacle to peace may rally the belligerents on the side of the one targeted.

A third way of securing the commitment of belligerent leaders is to guarantee their safety during the peace negotiation and its implementation. King succinctly illustrates this dilemma: "The prospect of war crime tribunals, the arrest of belligerent leaders and assigning blame for atrocities committed during the war all create disincentives for negotiations and generate equally strong incentives to renege on commitments during the implementation of a peace agreement" (ibid: 64).

King concludes that third parties can help alleviate the security concern of and generate trust among belligerents to enable them to search for their own solution, but the extent to which they can perform this role is a function of how the mediators are perceived by the factions as important yet powerful arbiters (ibid: 77-78). The foregoing analysis provides a very useful basis for assessing DfID and the British government's role in bringing an end to the conflict and in the post-war reconstruction phase in Sierra Leone.

2.7.   STUDIES ON POST-WAR RECONSTRUCTION

The topic of post-war reconstruction is widely discussed. Much of the substance of these debates is relevant to the discussion of what to do towards failed states and post- conflict situations today, reasons for shifting the current debate away from nation building and toward the concept of post-conflict reconstruction. For clarity, the World Bank's definition of post conflict reconstruction focuses on the needs for "the rebuilding of the socioeconomic framework of society" and the "reconstruction of the enabling conditions for a functioning peacetime society [to include] the framework of governance and rule of law" (World Bank 2003). For Kumar (1996) it focuses on rebuilding both formal and informal institutions, or more specifically, it involves the rebuilding of physical infrastructure and facilities, creation of minimal social services, and structural reform in the political, economic, and social and security sectors. 'Post-conflict' does not mean that conflict is concluded in all parts of a given country's territory. The term simply recognizes that most reconstruction tasks cannot be addressed until at least major parts of the country's territory have moved beyond conflict (ibid).

The general consensus from most of the literature on this issue is that using the term 'post-conflict reconstruction' is preferred to 'nation building' on the ground that it is context-specific, and unlike 'nation building', it provides what is needed to help reconstruct weak or failing states primarily after civil wars. Yarjah (2000) supports this view by outlining three reasons as to why 'post-conflict reconstruction' is preferable. His argument is as follows: first, post-conflict reconstruction recognizes the central role of local actors, "The citizens of the country in question will build their nation and bring about peace; outsiders can only support their efforts". Secondly, 'post-conflict reconstruction' emphasises the overcoming of conflict, "All societies and peoples must build their countries". Finally, 'post-war reconstruction', unlike 'nation building', carries less historical baggage. Despite the success of nation building in Japan, Germany, and Korea from 1945 to 1960, 'nation building', Yarjah argues, lost currency during the Vietnam War and is no longer fashionable.

Post-conflict reconstruction as it is conducted today comprises four distinct yet interrelated categories of tasks, or 'pillars.' These are security, justice and reconciliation, social and economic wellbeing, and governance and participation (Kumar 1998). Complementing these are reconstruction of physical infrastructure and repair of all kinds of material damage; rehabilitation of institutions and services; repatriation of returnees and relocation of internally displaced persons (IDPs); demobilization of combatants and reintegration of all war-affected groups of the population. However, reintegration can mean 'reinstating to an original state'. Reconstruction also, by and large, is a misleading notion. It also implies bringing societies back to those structures, which were to a large degree responsible for states gradually sliding to failure. If the original state was (part of) the cause of the original conflict, it is not wise to reinstate it. Following conflict, therefore, reintegration is likely to require the bringing together of the parties in different relationships or structures than previously. There may be a useful analogy in transplant surgery, where foreign body parts may be rejected unless there has been careful preparation, planning and sensitisation.

Indeed Kuhne (2001) observes that "reconstruction of roads, houses, infrastructure, government buildings, hospitals etc., is the easy part. The much more difficult one is that societies which have suffered from state failure need far reaching socio-cultural, economic and political transformation. Otherwise they are unable to generate sustainable, democratic, rule of law and good governance oriented state structures" (ibid).

With regard to reconciliation, whilst it implies promoting healing and harmony, it can also imply one or more parties becoming resigned or submissive to disagreeable outcomes (Azar 1990). People who continue to be marginalised have nothing to lose and may see potential gain from continued conflict. A holistic approach of necessity therefore should bring together different parties into a whole that offers opportunity for all. The term holistic can be defined (OED) as the tendency in nature to produce wholes from the orderly grouping of units, implying that the whole is greater than the sum of the parts and that all parts are important. This can be developed to mean an approach to post-war reconstruction and reintegration that creates opportunity for all parties – and not just for some.

2.8. FOUR PILLARS OF POST-WAR RECONSTRUCTION

2.8.1. SECURITY

It is arguable that aspects of public safety, in particular, creating a safe and secure environment and developing legitimate and effective security institutions are a precondition for development. This is vital since the process of social recovery should not be disrupted and set back by renewed outbreaks of violence. Security in this sense encompasses collective as well as individual security, which is also a precondition for achieving successful outcomes in the other pillars of post-conflict reconstruction (Gutkind 1943). In the most pressing sense, providing security involves securing the lives of civilians in the aftermath of immediate and large-scale violence as well as restoring the territorial integrity of the post-conflict government (Zartman 1995a). The reality of there having been a conflict, symbolized by a breakdown of law and order, begs for a security sector reform and the reorganization and training of the army and police as well as the placement of these institutions under the firm control of a democratically elected civilian leadership (Hagman 1996).

2.8.2   JUSTICE

The ending of overt violence via a peace agreement or military victory does not always mean the achievement of peace (Licklider 1993). Rather, the ending of violence or a so-called 'post-conflict' situation provides "a new set of opportunities that can be grasped or thrown away" (Luttwak 1999). Justice and order are important aspects of taking initiative in a post-conflict situation where there is a need to end violence, disarm combatants, restore the rule of law, and deal with the perpetrators of war crimes and other human rights abuses (Grant 2002). Public goods such as 'justice' are subjective and open to varying interpretations, and therefore escape quantification. But, if any lesson is to be learned from Sierra Leone's civil war and the preceding decades of poor governance, it is that sources of political, economic, and social grievances cannot be ignored.

The problem with this approach and how to deal with those accused of past human rights abuses and the question of amnesty or reconciliation is summed up by Bertram (1995: 387-418.) She claims that one of the most troubling quandaries for peace builders is that a policy of impunity or blanket amnesty creates ominous implications for UN efforts to build democracy and a sustainable peace. The need for reconciliation is in most post-war situations today considered to be either an antonym for the need for justice, or as competing objectives in the process of making and building peace. In the interest of reaching a settlement, alleged perpetrators of human rights abuses have often been included in negotiations, and, in some cases, even in the new governments. Sierra Leone is a prime example. However, as that case also demonstrates, Francis (2005) notes that "a peace agreement that allows power-sharing with criminals and amnesties for their crimes is perceived by the victims or survivors as an "unjust peace" and therefore "detrimental to post-war stability and reconciliation". Francis argues that such a structure "perpetuates a culture of impunity that fails to deter future war criminals, [and] it also fails to produce a just peace" (Francis 2005). The work concurs with Francis in that "issues of justice and accountability for war crimes and gross violations of human rights should not be glossed over in the civil war peace settlement" (ibid: 364) and that short-term pragmatism is not a recipe for long-term peace and stability (Lambourne 2004). More practically, justice should comprise the following:

1. **Apology:** Apology, if it is seen as a sign of genuine repentance and accompanied by some act of reparation or restitution, can play a part.

2. **Reparation:** Some sort of practical service or financial reparation may be required from those who have committed crimes to those who were their victims.

3. **Compensation:** Financial compensation from government, in the form of pensions.

4. **Punishment:** The punishment of those identified as particularly responsible can act as a sign of public imprisonment and acknowledgement, at the national or international level, that certain behaviours are intolerable, and may assuage the feelings of those who have suffered most (Kumar 1998).

2.8.3.   SOCIAL AND ECONOMIC WELLBEING

One factor that is often considered as contributing to or prohibiting a successful reconstruction is the politicization of ethnic homogeneity (Dobbins et al. 2003: 161-2). The historical results have been mixed: Japan and Germany are ethnically homogenous while Somalia, Haiti and Afghanistan are ethnically or clan-divided. However, fragmentation was also present in Bosnia and Kosovo, and they have achieved a level of stability although their reconstructions have not been completely successful.

In any case, it is not hetero- or homogeneity per se that leads to or prevents a successful reconstruction, but rather the ability of the populace to coordinate around the aims of the reconstruction. Indeed, a self-sustaining order requires the flexibility to handle heterogeneity on some margins. As the example of Japan illustrates, the order needs to be robust enough to handle the various views and beliefs of the populace at large. This is not to say that divisions within a society have no impact on the self-sustainability of the order, but rather that we cannot reach a general conclusion on the impact of heterogeneity. In other words, there is no guarantee that the reconstruction of a country where the populace is homogeneous on some margins will be successful and vice versa.

The economic condition of the post-war country also influences the post-war process. Japan and Germany had a well-established economic system prior to the U.S. occupation, which provided a foundation for the reconstruction process. In the first year after World War II, it is estimated that Japan's GDP was 50% of what it was in 1939 while Germany's GDP was about 75% of what is was in the pre-war period (Dobbins et al. 2003: 159-160). In countries such as Somalia and Haiti, major economic reforms were never undertaken. In these countries, an advanced exchange economy did not exist prior to reconstruction. The state of affairs remained one of widespread conflict, making the implementation of economic policies difficult. With that said, it is worth noting that however good an economic reconstruction programme is, in a state of anarchy it can be mired into a state of underdevelopment and stagnation. In short, good economic policies are a necessary, but not sufficient condition for success in post-war reconstruction.

2.8.4.   GOVERNANCE AND PARTICIPATION

Governance involves setting rules and procedures for political decision making and for delivering public services in an efficient and transparent manner, while participation encompasses the process of giving the population a voice in government by developing a civil society structure that generates and exchanges ideas through advocacy groups, civic associations, and the media. In attempting to carry out post-conflict reconstruction, a government may not be in a position to offer such political goods and, therefore, the goal for practitioners is to strengthen the political authority through the holding of elections. Grant (2002) agrees and reiterates further that, after a civil war, where the legitimacy of the incumbent government may be either questionable or fragile, democratic elections should be considered an essential first step.

However, the need for post-war reconstruction also overlooks the critical fact that elections in themselves do not necessarily yield (positive) results. "In the absence of supporting institutions," Coyne observes, "Elections can be counterproductive and actually impede the achievement of a successful reconstruction" (Coyne 1999). Zakaria (2003) notes that "The problem with democracies such as this is that they tend to promote the tyranny of the majority rather than the opposite". The election of Hitler in Germany or the election of military juntas in Chile, South Korea and Taiwan all serve to illustrate the point that democracy or having an election are not in themselves enough to obtain the desired outcome". Based on the lessons learned from the above examples, one can then theorise that if elections take place in the absence of the basic infrastructure for democracy survival, the reconstruction may very well fail. Democracy can only be effective when citizens are committed to it. Without this commitment, democracy can bring tyranny and chaos.

2.9.   CONCLUSION

A theoretical framework provides the basis for understanding the dynamics of civil wars and for the evaluation of peace processes. The presented theories and studies cover different phases and aspects of conflict resolution: from the causes to conflict management up to post-conflict reconstruction. The human needs theory focuses on the denial of the provision of human needs such as security and participation to some groups, which, according to Burton, lay at the core of conflict. The underlying causes of a conflict have to be taken into account in order for a peace settlement to be a lasting solution to the conflict. Stedman notes that the resolution of a conflict is challenging as one has to deal with two levels – the underlying conflict causes and the concerns resulting from war such as security and survival. Bad leadership, a strong sense of antagonistic history, and mounting economic problems – Brown's causes of internal conflict are all potentially relevant for the Sierra Leonean case study. The concerns that are directly resulting from war activities can become even more important during the peace negotiations and shortly after the signing of a peace agreement as the combatants want their physical and financial security to be ensured during peace time. According to King, third parties can play a major role in helping to generate trust among warring factions and to alleviate their security concerns. They can, furthermore, help to circumvent the structural obstacles to resolving internal conflicts such as asymmetry in commitment of the warring factions, and promote a durable negotiated settlement. As the focus is on post-conflict reconstruction, the last part of Chapter Two introduces the concept of post-conflict reconstruction. For Kumar, post-conflict reconstruction involves the rebuilding of both formal and informal institutions – rebuilding of infrastructure, creation of social services, and structural reforms. The four pillars security, justice and reconciliation, social and economic wellbeing, and governance and participation comprise all important sectors of post-conflict reconstruction and will be revisited in the following chapters, applying the relevant theories and concepts to the Sierra Leonean case study.

The case of Sierra Leone indicates that policymakers need to rethink both the widely accepted characteristics of weak and failed states, and the feasible policy prescriptions available to the international community in dealing with them. The misdiagnosis of the Sierra Leone conflict, as the next chapter will show, led to policies and interventions which resulted in ineffective and perverse outcomes.

$$\boxed{\ \mathbf{3}\ }$$

EVOLUTION AND DEVELOPMENT

THE EVOLUTION AND DEVELOPMENT OF CIVIL WAR IN SIERRA LEONE

3.1. INTRODUCTION

In his human needs theory, Burton (1990a) postulates that if societies are to remain significantly free of conflict, development needs must be catered for. Whereas an individual is responsive to opportunities for the improvement of his/her life style, he/she refuses to accept the denial of ontological needs like security, dignity etc. As a result, any political system that denies or suppresses these human needs eventually generates protest or conflict. This remains Burton's first law of conflict and will to a large extent form the basis of this study.

Without making excuses for the inhumane activities that took place, it can be argued that the denial of ontological needs manifested itself in Sierra Leone by the amputation of limbs and hands and with human beings seeking to harm each other. Because of this, we require more convincing explanations with less room for the unknown, while avoiding the temptation to describe the violence as pathological without understanding the reasons that bred it.

This chapter addresses the historical evolution of the state, and Sierra Leone's social, political economic development under colonial rule, the first few years of independence, the conflict period, and the attempts that were made to resolve it.

3.2. COLONIAL RULE AND THE POST-INDEPENDENCE SIERRA LEONE

By 1821 Freetown had become so prominent that other colonies such as the Gold Coast were placed under the governor of Sierra Leone. In 1863 an advisory legislative council was established in Sierra Leone. The British were reluctant to assume added responsibility by increasing the size of the colony, but in 1896 the interior was proclaimed a British protectorate and the Colony and Protectorate of Sierra Leone was established. The protectorate was ruled "indirectly" (i.e., through the rulers of the numerous small states, rather than by creating an entirely new administrative structure) and a hut tax was imposed in 1898 to pay for administrative costs. In 1889, Bai Bureh and other chiefs in the interior and the Poro secret society in the South waged the Hut Tax War. The British, although well equipped, did not achieve an easy victory over these opposing, well-determined indigenous people. The Colonial government suspected the Creoles of causing the conflict, and as a consequence, the Creoles found themselves being excluded from trade and commerce in favour of the Lebanese. This led to a constitution adopted in 1951 that gave additional power to Chiefs, most of whom were put in power by the Colonial government. With the Creoles being a small minority in the combined colony and protectorate, it was not surprising that they were defeated in the elections of 1951, which were won by the protectorate-based Sierra Leone People's Party (SLPP), led by Dr. Milton Margai (a Mende).

On April 27, 1961, Sierra Leone became independent, with Margai as prime minister. He died in 1964. He was succeeded by his brother, Albert M. Margai. Following the 1967 general elections, Siaka Stevens of the All People's Congress (APC) party, a Temne-based party was appointed prime minister by the governor-general (a Sierra Leonean who represented the British monarch). However, a military coup led by Brigadier David Lansana in support of Margai ousted Stevens a few minutes after he took the oath of office.

The Lansana government itself was soon toppled and replaced by a National Reformation Council (NRC), headed by Col. Andrew Juxom-Smith. In 1968, an army revolt overthrew the NRC and returned the nation to parliamentary government, with Stevens as prime minister. The following years were marked by considerable unrest, caused by ethnic and army disaffection with the central government. After an attempted coup in 1971, parliament declared Sierra Leone to be a republic with Stevens as president.

3.3.   SIAKA STEVENS' NEO-PATRIMONIAL STATE

Already a weak creation of colonization and decolonization, state collapse took place under the long reign of Siaka Stevens (1968-85) and his All People's Congress (APC) Party. The Party drew its support primarily on the interior Temne and Limba people from the northern part of the country, reacting against the previous predominance of the coastal Mende people from the South and East (Reno 1995). Stevens introduced warlord politics to Sierra Leone. By warlord politics, Reno (1995) meant "attempts made by rulers to control, using non economic and bureaucratic means to enhance their own power rather than the state". Putting that into context, Siaka Stevens' rule can be seen as the perfect example of warlord politics.

President Stevens systematically reduced Sierra Leone's capability to govern its territory in order to maximize his own personal power. To this end, Stevens "sold chances to profit to those who could pay for it through provision of services" (ibid). He created a private military force to terrorize his own people and to aggrandize himself, especially in the diamond fields. As the official rule of law receded, the law of the jungle, presided over by Stevens, took its place. State Institutions were either broken down or corrupted. The state became entangled in a civil war, fought primarily over the remnants of his reign, encouraged and assisted by 'invisible hands'.

Siaka Stevens' neo-patrimonial state was not about development; it was about enriching himself and a small group of followers (Reno 1995). The state services were up for sale to the highest bidder in a context of patron-client relationships (Chege 2002). It is also said that the state autonomy required for development is autonomy from classes and groups involved in zero-sum activities, that is, speculation, corruption, usury and the like. In Sierra Leone, those groups were Siaka Stevens himself and his clique. The state elite were thus part of the development problem and not at all part of the solution (TRC Volume 3a).

Having looted an estimated $500 million and leaving a balance of barely $196,000 in foreign reserves in the Bank of Sierra Leone on the day he left office, Stevens retired in 1985 and   designating the army chief, Major General Joseph Saidu Momoh, as his successor. It was under Momoh, Stevens's handpicked, inept successor, that state collapse was consummated. Gen. Joseph Momoh, a former military officer, was even less skilled in statecraft than was Stevens. Momoh remained in power until 1992. Public institutions were already a hollow ineffective sham compared to what they had been in the 1960s (Pham 2006). At one point in 1986, Pham observed, "it even hosted a state visit by Yasir Arafat who was just driven out of Beirut by the Israeli army. They contemplated making a quick $8million by selling to the Palestinian leader an island on which to regroup his forces" (Pham 2001). In another scenario, as Charles Taylor attempted to launch his invasion from Sierra Leone into Liberia, Taylor travelled to Sierra Leone and offered to pay Momoh but as Ellis succinctly observed in his study of the Liberian civil conflict: "The notoriously venal Momoh promptly sought from [then Liberian president] Samuel Doe a higher sum, turning the approach into an auction, an action for which his country was later to pay dearly" (Ellis 1996).

In the public's eye, the state lacked legitimacy. Corruption and illegality became the source of livelihood, as public educational and the health services vanished. It was in Momoh's reign that the tinder for the conflict began to gather. In 1987 the government stopped paying salaries, notably to schoolteachers and the military (Hayward 1989). Structures of authority disintegrated (Clapham 1998); unemployed youth wandered the streets of Freetown and the interior and took to drugs and petty crime; soldiers turned to brigandage. Disaffected soldiers were the political entrepreneurs who put the match to the tinder.

3.4.   RUF INVASION

The Liberian conflict had direct effects on neighbouring Sierra Leone: it was believed that Taylor never forgave Momoh for not allowing him to use Sierra Leone as his launching pad and just as he was on the verge of victory in early 1990, the Economic Community of West African States (ECOWAS), decided to intervene in the Liberian conflict with its own ECOWAS Monitoring Group (ECOMOG). As Francis, observed "Momoh not only permitted ECOMOG to use the Lungi International Airport, near Freetown, to bomb areas in Liberia controlled by Taylor's rebels, but sent Sierra Leonean units to join the intervention force" (Francis 2006).

It was because of this resentment against the Momoh regime that Taylor decided to assist a group of dissidents alleged to have gone to Libya to train to overthrow the corrupt and venal Momoh government. He then helped form the RUF under Colonel Foday Sankoh, a charismatic former Sierra Leonean army corporal who had been jailed for several years in the 1970s for his alleged role in the failed 1971 revolt against the Stevens' regime. This was to force the government of Sierra Leone to withdraw its troops from Liberia. Taylor, by forming and supporting the RUF, wanted to pressure the Sierra Leone government into withdrawing its support from ECOMOG (Abdullah 2004).

The government of Sierra Leone overwhelmed by corruption and a crumbling economy, was unable to put up a significant resistance. Within a month of entering the region from Kailahun, the RUF overran much of the eastern part of the country (Abdullah 2004: 207–208). Following up on its initial success, the RUF targeted economic centres and diamond mines in the south-eastern and south-western parts of the country. At first, the RUF ostensibly fought for a redress of the iniquities of Sierra Leonean society. The APC regime exploited the rich diamond resources for the sole benefit of its elite in the face of the low living standards in the country.

The RUF first displayed some of its brutal tactics and attacks on civilians and carried out public executions of minority ethnic groups. These were attempts to emulate Taylor's successful tactics of ethnic incitement in Liberia. The RUF murdered more than a hundred Fulani and Madingo traders in its first two months of operations (Francis 2005). Soon people who had been displaced began to flee towards the Sierra Leonean capital Freetown. The RUF had two major calling cards: dead civilians; and hundreds, possibly thousands, of living civilians with their limbs crudely amputated.

By January 1995, facing demoralized and under-equipped government troops, the RUF controlled the three most important mining operations in the country, including the Koidu diamond area. Rebel troops now controlled territories only miles from the capital, Freetown. Faced with imminent defeat and the inability of government troops to hold off the RUF, the government of Sierra Leone turned to the South African company Executive Outcomes (EO), staffed by many former members of the South African Defence Force (SADF). Hiring EO brought some immediate results; the RUF was swiftly beaten back from the capital, and within a month the government regained control of the diamond producing areas. It is worth noting that EO operations were partly financed by the diamond operations in Sierra Leone. Swift series of defeats and the loss of control of important mining regions brought the RUF to the negotiating table (Pham 2006).

3.5.   NPRC (FROM PROTEST TO COUP D'ETAT)

With the government not paying salaries to the military, structures of authority disintegrated. However, despite the wide level of corruption, the government won increasing support from donors throughout the 1980s, perhaps, as Hanlon observed, "Because it was also faithfully introducing IMF policies such as devaluation" (cited in Gberie 2005). As a result of the non-payment of salaries, dissatisfied junior officers led by Captain Valentine Strasser in April 1992 came to Freetown to protest against their current situation. Within a day, this protest led to a coup. Members of the armed forces seized the Sierra Leone Broadcasting Station (SLBS), occupied the presidential offices and installed a five-member military junta under 27-year-old Captain Valentine Strasser. Momoh was forced to flee to Guinea and Strasser announced the formation of a National Provisional Ruling Council (NPRC) (Kaplan 1994). The current president of Sierra Leone, Ahmad Tejan Kabbah, then a senior official with the United Nations Development Programme, offered his services to the young *putschists* and became the chairman of their national advisory council (Pham 2006).

On assuming power, the NPRC claimed an expeditious end to the war as one of its principal aims, and exploring unique opportunities to open dialogue with the RUF. By the time of the coup, the RUF had been confined to remote areas of Kailahun District in the east of the country and Pujehun in the south. The NPRC's anti-corruption and anti-elite rhetoric was popular across the country and appeared to be in tune with the RUF's own pronouncements. Expectations that the coup offered prospects for a peaceful end to the war were raised in the first week, when RUF spokesmen broadcast messages through the BBC announcing a unilateral ceasefire and a readiness to work with the NPRC in the interest of 'peace and reconciliation'. Both sides celebrated what they saw as an end to a repressive and corrupt era.

However, this promising start to peace did not gain momentum. The NPRC vacillated in dealing with the RUF, and publicly offering an amnesty in return for unconditional surrender without initiating further overtures. Meanwhile, Strasser dismissed the RUF in much the same terms as Momoh referred to them as "bandits sent by Charles Taylor" to wreak havoc in Sierra Leone

(Gberie 2005). In retrospect, Strasser's successor, Julius Maada Bio, said the young soldiers had convinced themselves that, with the resources of the state at their disposal, they would – and should – easily crush the RUF rebels, rather than negotiate and share power with them.

In October 1992 the RUF were to prove the NPRC wrong by taking over Kono, the principal mining town (Abdullah 1998). As a result of this and with pressure from the international community for a negotiated settlement and a return to democracy in November 1993, Strasser issued a timetable for a transition to democracy to culminate in general elections in late 1995. A month later, the NPRC released a "Working Document on the Constitution" to serve as the basis for public debates leading to a constitutional referendum in May 1995 (Hirsch 2001: 153.) However, before this could happen, Strasser's deputy, Brigadier General Julius Maada Bio ousted him in 1996 and provided him with a safe exit out of the country. Unlike other African leaders, Strasser faced a kinder fate, with his safe exit out of Sierra Leone and into the UK. A scholarship was procured for him by the British government - funded by the United Nations to study at Warwick University. His academic career was short-lived: the military ruler-turned-scholar was recognized by a fellow student from Sierra Leone and ensuing campus protests led to his removal.

The new leader, Bio, under increasing foreign and domestic pressure, was forced to hold elections, which were boycotted and sporadically disrupted by the RUF. James Jonah, a colleague of Kabbah at the United Nations, was appointed Chairman for the Electoral Commission and after Tejan Kabbah's election victory, was made minister of finance. Bio's greatest achievement was the re-launching of negotiations with the rural rebellion and handing over power to Kabbah in March 1996. Tejan Kabbah continued negotiations begun by Bio and made substantial concessions to the rebels that paved the way for the Abidjan Agreement of November 1996.

3.6.   THE FAILED 1996 ELECTION

After the successful 1996 ceasefire in Sierra Leone, Britain and the United States pushed hard for early elections. The three main reasons for this were that, firstly, they backed Kabbah whom they knew would likely be elected; secondly, they refused to accept the RUF in a transitional government; and finally, they wanted to speed up their own exits from the country (ICG 2001). In choosing this strategy, the international community and institutions and/or their representatives forgot about the most important aspect of the conflict, the peace process, and the establishment of dialogue with the rebels (Hirsch 2001).

The outcome was that presidential and parliamentary elections were held in February 1996, even though they were violently opposed by rebel forces, resulting in 27 deaths. Neither candidate—Ahmad Tejan Kabbah (Sierra Leone People's Party) nor Dr. John Karefa-Smart of the United National People's Party (UNPP)—received a majority of the vote, and a run-off election was held on 15 March 1996. Kabbah won the election with 59.4 per cent of the vote but he remained president of Sierra Leone for only 14 months. In May 1997, he was toppled by the army, led by Major Johnny Paul Koroma, who formed the Armed Forces Revolutionary Council (AFRC) on 25 May 1997 and promptly made common cause with the rebels.

The subsequent decade after the first cease fire and coup saw a battle for control over the capital and the rest of the country by various loyal and dissident military and rebel groups. Kabbah was restored to power ten months later and was again chased out of the capital for several months in early 1999, before being restored once again. During this period, a legitimate civilian government was in place (scarcely in power) from the March 1996 elections until the May 1997 coup, from March 1998 until the end of the year, and again after the spring of 1999 – for a period of four years.

3.7.   THE ARMED FORCES REVOLUTIONARY COUNCIL

The Armed Forces Revolutionary Council (AFRC) was formed on the 25 of May 1997. With the signing of the Abidjan Peace Accord and with the RUF appearing to have been defeated, President Ahmad Tejan Kabbah ended the contract with EO (Mills 1999). This was followed by a string of reforms, dealt with separately in the analysis section in chapter six. The army staged their first coup, which caused Kabbah to flee the country and the Armed Forces Revolutionary Council (AFRC), with Major Koroma at its head, assumed control of Freetown. Koroma declared an end to the war and the AFRC invited the RUF to share power. The RUF was given free access to the capital, all anti-government demonstrations were banned and political parties were abolished. Images and reports of widespread looting, rape, and murder soon revealed the horror of the situation to the world. The period of AFRC/RUF control of Freetown resulted in chaos, referred to by the RUF as "Operation Pay Yourself" (Phillips 2003).

This prompted the Commonwealth to suspend Sierra Leone's membership in July 1997, and on 8 October 1997 the United Nations Security Council imposed sanctions against Sierra Leone, barring the supply of arms and petroleum products to Sierra Leone (ibid: 73). By September 1997 fierce fighting had broken out between junta soldiers and the West African peacekeeping troops: The Nigerian-led ECOMOG force returned to battle with the AFRC/RUF for control of Freetown. By the February of 1998 the AFRC/RUF was forced out, restoring President Kabbah to power, and the leader of the RUF, Foday Sankoh, was arrested in Nigeria and returned to Freetown. Pursued by ECOMOG, the AFRC/RUF returned to the countryside (Oludipe 2000). A broken force, the RUF then began a systematic campaign of murder, mutilation, kidnapping and, terrorizing the countryside under an operation known as "Operation No Living Thing" (Radio Netherlands 21 January 2000).

Subsequently, the AFRC/RUF infiltrated forces into Freetown catching ECOMOG by surprise. The result was another brutal battle in Freetown as ECOMOG and RUF forces fought for control in January 1999. Britain was urgently training Sierra Leonean troops, while US Special Forces were training Nigerian battalions for peacekeeping duties in Sierra Leone. It was at this juncture that momentum began building up in the international community to negotiate peace between the rebels and the government, and a United Nations peacekeeping force was sent. At the end of 1999 UN peacekeepers began arriving in Sierra Leone. Currently, (2008) UN peacekeepers with support from British forces have helped to restore some stability and relative peace to Sierra Leone after several failed peace agreements between the rebels and the Sierra Leone government. The RUF leader died in captivity. However, the country has yet to return to complete normality.

3.8.   CONFLICT AGENDAS AND MILITARY DEADLOCKS

External intervention to contain the conflict was carried out by four agents: the essentially Nigerian-led force of the Military Observer Group (ECOMOG); the Economic Community of West African States (ECOWAS); the United Nations Observer/Armed Mission in Sierra Leone (UNOMSIL/UNAMSIL); and the British Army (Fowler 2005). Three peace agreements were signed as a result of these efforts: the Abidjan Accord of November 1996 (Garcia 1997), the Conakry Peace Plan of October 1997 (Ibid), and the Lome Peace Agreement of July 1999. The West African peacekeeping force ECOMOG entered Sierra Leone in 1995 to help the NPRC and, later, the Kabbah government to fight the RUF rebels. After the

May 25, 1997 military coup of the AFRC, and its establishment of a coalition government with RUF rebels, hundreds of additional Nigerian soldiers assigned to ECOMOG in Liberia moved to Sierra Leone to defend Freetown airport. The civil defence forces, especially the Kamajors, also assisted the ousted SLPP government.

3.9.   WEST AFRICAN RESPONSE

3.9.1.   ECOWAS

The inauguration of ECOWAS in 1975 should be seen as the culmination of several attempts over a period of one and a half decades (from 1960 when most West African states gained independence) to form a sub-regional organization embracing the whole of West Africa. Initial attempts had floundered firstly as a result of the rivalry between Ghana (under Kwame Nkrumah) and Nigeria (under Tafawa Balewa) in the early 1960s and later the struggle for supremacy in the sub-region between Nigeria and Cote d'Ivoire along Anglophone-Francophone lines.

Most of these rivalries were put aside and by 1975 the first treaty was signed, ushering in the passage of more treaties. These include the ECOWAS Treaty of 1975, the ECOWAS Protocol on Non-Aggression, signed in 1978 in Lagos, and the ECOWAS Protocol Relating to Mutual Assistance on Defence (MAD) (Conteh-Morgan/Magyar 1998). The Treaty of 1975, which created ECOWAS, envisaged an economic community which aimed at promoting "[c]o-operation and development in all fields of economic activity … and in social and cultural matters for the purpose of raising the standard of living of its peoples, of increasing and maintaining economic stability of fostering closer relations among its members and of contributing to the progress and development of the African continent" (ibid).

The ECOWAS MAD Protocol was signed in May 1981 at the Freetown summit two years after it had been proposed by Senegal and Togo. But it is significant to note (as would become common place with issues relating to ECOWAS' role in Liberia), that the defence pact proposal was vehemently opposed by such member states as Mali, Guinea-Bissau and Cape Verde (Adebajo 2002). This highlights that the establishment of an economic union should have in it defence implications that transcend national (or territorial) boundaries (Adebajo 1999). The protection of joint services as well as industrial and economic ventures jointly owned could not be left in the hands of the individual states, especially (as in the case of ECOWAS) as some of its members are too weak to protect themselves. Under such circumstances a common security arrangement becomes necessary. It was against this background that the ECOWAS Non-Aggression Pact was signed.

In its preamble, ECOWAS leaders admitted that the community "can attain its objective save in an atmosphere of peace and harmonious understanding, among its members. The protocol, therefore, demands *inter alia* that members refrain from threats or the use of force against the territorial integrity of the political independence of other members states; refrain from committing, encouraging or condoning acts of subversion; and prevent the use of their territories as bases for launching subversion; and also to "respond to all peaceful means in the settlement of disputes arising among themselves" (Olonisakin 2000). While the agreement on non-aggression created a friendly atmosphere and generated trust among it members, it was inadequate in addressing external aggression or externally supported domestic insurrection and revolt. It was to cater for this inadequacy that the Protocol relating to Mutual Assistance on Defence came into being.

3.9.2. ECOWAS PROTOCOL RELATING TO MUTUAL ASSISTANCE ON DEFENCE (MAD)

Articles 2 and 3 adopted the principles of collective security and collective defence respectively. In article 2, any armed threat or aggression against any member state was to be considered as one against the entire community; and Article 3 required member states to give mutual aid and assistance to members affected.

The protocol provided further that units from the armies of ECOWAS countries would constitute ad-hoc Allied Armed Forces of the Community (AAFC), in case of an emergency. It therefore did not create a permanent ECOWAS standing army. This would mean that when the time came for ECOWAS to enter Liberia, unlike NATO, there were no standby units, and ECOMOG had to rely solely on personnel contributed on a voluntary basis by some member states.

The AAFC task was to carry out joint military exercises. It was placed under the command of a Force Commander appointed by the ECOWAS Authority and who together with the Chief of Defence Staff of the assisted state was to implement the decisions of the Authority. The actions of the

Force Commander were to be subject to the competent authority of the member state or states concerned.

This last provision could easily be applied in situations of external threat against a member state. In the case of internal conflict in a failed state (for instance, Liberia) the provision could create problems since there would be no competent political authority – a problem to confront the first ECOMOG Commander in Liberia.

The protocol also provided for a Defence Council comprising ministers of defence and foreign affairs of member states under the current chairmanship of ECOWAS. In addition, the Chiefs of Defence Staff of member states were to constitute the Defence Commission with the responsibility of examining the technical aspects of defence. Article 12 provided for the appointment of a Deputy-Executive Secretary for military affairs whose functions included updating plans for the movement of troops and logistics, initiating joint exercises and managing the military budget of the secretariat. These observations among others, do not deny the fact that together, the protocols on Non-Aggression and Mutual Assistance on Defence provided some legal basis for ECOWAS' intervention in Sierra Leone.

3.9.3. ECOMOG IN SIERRA LEONE

A small ECOMOG unit has been in Sierra Leone since the mid-1990s. Their initial role was to assist Sierra Leone when it was clear that Charles Taylor was helping the RUF. This small unit was restricted to guarding key installations. Their full involvement in the conflict came in 1998 when they were mandated by Ministers of Foreign Affairs from ECOWAS countries and supported by the Organisation of African Unity (OAU) to reinstate the elected government of President Tejan Kabbah. A ministerial committee was formed to monitor the situation in Sierra Leone in 1998 as ordered by the OAU heads of state. ECOMOG forces under the command of a Nigerian general were supported by yet another mercenary outfit— the British-based firm Sandline International—hired by the exiled then President Kabbah. ECOMOG and Sandline launched an offensive against the combined AFRC/RUF forces in February 1998 that eventually restored Kabbah to power the following month (Pham 2006).

The following year, in January 1999 the AFRC/RUF forces returned to Freetown, taking ECOMOG by surprise and forcing Kabbah to flee the country once more. The result was another brutal battle in Freetown as

ECOMOG and RUF forces fought for control. This was not to last for long as ECOMOG forces, with reinforcement from Nigeria, returned to battle and recaptured the Capital city. The fight for the capital city cost the lives of some 7,000 civilians and two-thirds of the city destroyed (Kaplan 2001).

The resurgence of the RUF brought a realisation that the war could not be won militarily, and this forced president Kabbah and his Nigerian backers to enter into negotiations. Pham observes that the fighting claimed estimated 800 peacekeepers and cost them about $1 million daily. This forced the two Sierra Leonean parties to enter into negotiations which resulted in the July 7, 1999, Lomé Peace Agreement.

3.10.   CIVIL DEFENCE FORCES (CDF)

The Civil Defence Forces were another major player in the civil war. They have their origin in traditional hunters and secret societies. In the South they called themselves the Kamajors (Muana 1997) and are also referred to as the Tamamboroh in the North and the North-East of Sierra Leone. These traditional warriors differ to a large extent by culture, aims and objectives and thus avoid fighting together but remain connected by a common cause.

Both civil defence forces originated from the secret societies which historically had been the setting in which young men were trained to defend their community. But as Bona recounts, they also "function as educational centres (including sex education). The societies for men in the South and East of Sierra Leone are called Poro while in the North are the Gbanbani and the Soko; the ones for women are called Bundo" (Bona 2000). They are responsible for initiation rituals by which boys and girls become accepted as full men or women. Traditionally, these have the power to declare war. Due to these multiple functions, the secret societies, which amalgated with Civil Defence Forces such as the Kamajor and Tamanboroh, soon became a force for the RUF to contend with.

However, unlike the Tamamboroh who remain out of politics, the leader of the Kamajors was the Minister of Defence, and because the Kamajors originated from the South and East of the country, a SLPP stronghold, they soon became more or less a gang carrying out the 'dirty work' of the SLPP. With political backing from Freetown and later from Guinea when the government was deposed, the Kamajors set up checkpoints between Bo and Kenema harassing travellers and killing those they suspected of belonging to the RUF. In Freetown they took over hotels and went about in daylight lynching those whom they thought gave out RUF odour (Muana 2000). Their attitude made it very difficult for people from the North to come to the South. The Temne had problems with the CDF in the areas under their control. Even though commentators such as Chege note that Sierra Leone did not experience the ethnic fratricide often blamed for state collapse, it was clear that ethnicity was an issue. However, that part of the conflict was swept under the carpet, because of the barbarity of the RUF.

3.11.   THE ABIDJAN ACCORD (1996)

The election of a civilian government in 1996 undermined any legitimacy the RUF might have claimed and relegated it to an insurgent threat. Further, with the assault of EO and the Kamajors, supported by the SLA, on the RUF positions and the destruction of the RUF headquarters southeast of Kenema in November 1996, Foday Sankoh agreed to sign the Abidjan peace accord. A senior diplomat in Freetown noted that, 'always military pressure was needed to be put on before negotiations could succeed'.

It was no surprise that a pre-condition imposed by Foday Sankoh for negotiation and a cease fire was the removal of EO from Sierra Leone. Unwisely, Tejan Kabbah agreed. In its place a UN peacekeeping force was to be established. However, it never arrived. Donors were not willing to meet the U.S. $47 million bill for 700 soldiers, and Sankoh continued to dispute the agreement, maintaining that the UN presence should be less than 100. Nevertheless, EO was finally asked to leave by President Kabbah, who believed the RUF was sincere about peace. Three months later, without any external force to defend his government, he was deposed in another military coup led by the Armed Forces Revolutionary Council (AFRC).

However, in the annual summit meeting of the heads of state and government of the Organization of African Unity (OAU) in Harare, Zimbabwe, just a day after the 1997 coup, the leaders present at the meeting, who as Pham (2006) observes, "had themselves come to power through military coups and in contrast to the OAU's usual practice of non-interference in the internal affairs of member state", called for "the immediate restoration of constitutional order" in Sierra Leone and urged "all African countries and the international community at large to refrain from recognizing the new regime and lending support in any form whatsoever to the perpetrators of the *coup d'état*". The leaders of ECOWAS to assist the people of Sierra Leone to restore constitutional order to the country and to implement the Abidjan Agreement which continues to serve as a viable framework for peace, stability and reconciliation in Sierra Leone" (McEvoy-Levy 2006).

3.12.   THE CONAKRY ACCORD (1997)

The AFRC regime was not recognized by any foreign government or by the Sierra Leone people. After extensive bloodshed and destruction, the Conakry Accord was signed in October 1997 by a delegation sent by the AFRC leader Johnny Paul Koroma. It was intended to restore the Kabbah government. But it clearly became a ploy to buy time in the face of international pressure and a domestic boycott by government employees, who refused to work under the AFRC regime and shut down key government functions. Under cover of the accord, the AFRC stockpiled weapons and attacked remaining ECOMOG positions at the country's international airport at Lungi (Garcia 1997).

3.13.   THE LOME ACCORD (25 MAY 1999 to 7 JULY 1999)

The January occupation of Freetown brought a realisation to both parties to the conflict that it could not be won militarily. In March 1999, President Kabbah visited several key countries in the sub-region, including Côte d'Ivoire, Ghana, Nigeria, and Togo to discuss the situation in Sierra Leone and possible ways forward. This was a complete reversal of the path formerly followed of trying to defeat and kill the RUF rebels. Present at these talks were the ECOMOG troop-contributing countries, namely Nigeria, Guinea, Ghana, and Mali. The governments of the UK and the USA (the USA being represented by the United States presidential special envoy for the promotion of democracy in Africa, the Rev. Jesse Jackson); and the UN Secretary-General's special representative for Sierra Leone, Francis G. Okelo.

In their presence on May 18 1999, the Sierra Leonean government and the RUF signed a cease-fire agreement, which came into effect on May 24, 1999. Under the agreement, both parties were to maintain their respective positions and refrain from hostile or aggressive acts. On June 2, 1999, the government and the RUF decided to ask UNOMSIL to establish a committee to effect the immediate release of prisoners of war and non-combatants in accordance with the May 18 cease-fire agreement. The agreement also achieved one of RUF's central goals – the RUF was brought into the government, gaining four cabinet positions. It also headed a number of public sector directorships and filled some ambassadorial posts. The exit of the Nigerian peacekeeping troops was also achieved.

Foday Sankoh was rewarded with the status of vice president and chairmanship of the Strategic Mineral Resources Commission, effectively giving him access to the country's diamond resources. Under the Lome agreement, and most controversially, there was a blanket amnesty for all crimes committed during the war, however terrible (ICG 2002). The accord also promised the rebel leader and his followers a "complete amnesty for any crimes committed...from March 1991 up to the date of the agreement."

Indeed, it was the Lomé Peace Accord that effectively ended the war. Although there were some hitches such as a return to hostilities when some UN soldiers were captured by a group of RUF fighters culminating in the shooting down of some 20 demonstrators at the residence of RUF leader Foday Sankoh.

3.14.   UNITED NATIONS' RESPONSE

The United Nations' initial reaction to the 1997 military coup by the Armed Forces Revolutionary Council (AFRC) was to condemn it and to place sanctions against the government formed by the rebels. The United Nations Security Council commended ECOWAS on its efforts to restore the ousted government of President Tejan Kabbah and urged member states to assist ECOMOG with financial and logistical support. It also condemned the atrocities perpetrated by the rebels, particularly against women and children.

In July 1998, the UN Security Council unanimously approved a resolution to establish the United Nations Observer Mission to Sierra Leone (UNOMSIL) and a 6,000-strong UN Armed Mission in Sierra Leone (UNAMSIL) (Dobbins 2005). Their responsibility as spelled out by the UN was "to monitor and help ECOMOG with the implementation of a program for the disarmament, demobilization, and reintegration of combatants (the DDR program); reporting on the security situation; monitoring respect for international humanitarian law, including at disarmament and demobilization sites; and advising the government of Sierra Leone and local police officials on police practice, training, re-equipment, and recruitment, in particular on the need to respect internationally accepted standards of policing in democratic societies"(UN Resolution 1181, July 13, 1998; cited by Human Rights Watch 1999).

However in late 1999 and early 2000, UN peacekeepers were themselves disarmed by RUF forces. The situation deteriorated in early May 2000 when the RUF killed seven UN peacekeepers and captured fifty others. The number of peacekeepers taken prisoners by the RUF increased to over 500 as the UN forces, under the command of Indian Major General Vijay Kumar Jetley, who was experiencing difficulties with the Nigerian component of his command, apparently surrendered to the rebels without firing a shot (Pham 2005). This prompted the Security Council to increase UNAMSIL's personnel to 11,100 and later to 17,500, the largest UN peacekeeping operation in the world at the time. UNAMSIL's mission was revised to include protecting the government of President Kabbah. Additionally, "the main objectives of UNAMSIL in Sierra Leone remains to assist the efforts of the government of Sierra Leone to extend its authority, restore law and order and stabilize the situation progressively throughout the entire country and finally to assist in the promotion of a political process which should lead to a renewed disarmament, demobilization and reintegration program and the holding, in due course, of free and fair elections." (United Nations 2001).

On January 14, 2002, the commander of UNAMSIL, General Daniel Opande, declared the Sierra Leone war officially over after the surrender of some 45,000 demobilized rebels of the RUF, Kamajor militias, and armed gangs called the "West Side Boys," and renegade soldiers of what remained of the Sierra Leonean army. Today, UN peacekeepers, with support from British forces, have helped to restore some stability and relative peace to Sierra Leone after several failed peace agreements between the rebels and the Sierra Leone government. The RUF leader died in captivity.

3.15.   THE ROLE OF THE UNITED KINGDOM

The United Kingdom has maintained an interest in Sierra Leone since independence and remains committed to the country today. It contributed the bulk of the funding to the February 1996 election earlier. The so-called Sandline Affair (known also as the 'Arms to Africa Affair') and the publicity surrounding atrocities in Sierra Leone intensified British's interest. In March 1998 it was reported that the British private security company Sandline (an associate of Executive Outcomes) had violated an arms embargo on Sierra Leone. Sandline had purchased weapons and provided a small number of personnel and a helicopter in support of the February 1998 Nigerian assault on Freetown to reinstate President Kabbah. Sandline dubbed 'mercenaries' in the British press claimed that the UK government had prior knowledge of its intention to assist Kabbah. While the Labour government condemned the affair as an affront to ethical foreign policy, it appeared to many that the company was supporting the restoration of democracy against a barbarous AFRC/RUF junta and could, therefore, be seen as being on the 'right' side in Sierra Leone's war.

Sandline's intervention raised a more fundamental issue. In the absence of other international assistance, President Kabbah had little choice other than to arrange a commercial deal to obtain the funds to pay Sandline for its support and to request the help of Nigeria, which then was under the dictatorial rule of Sani Abacha. The international media coverage of atrocities by the RUF in Freetown in January 1999 fuelled further pressure on the UK to assist in resolution of the Sierra Leone conflict. These events resulted in a marked increase of UK funds to restructure the Sierra Leone armed forces in 1999. As noted earlier, the UK's policy to train and equip SLA troops to inflict a military defeat on the RUF was a high-risk. A military offensive against the RUF might have been essential given the failure of Sierra Leone's elected government to stabilise the country and end the war. However, if pursued in the absence of an appropriate political strategy it could have proved disastrous. Even if a reorganized SLA, supported by British troops, could have decisively defeated the RUF, the consequence might have resulted in further regional destabilisation since RUF forces could regroup in Liberia and renew their offensive in Guinea. Moreover, SLA forces, unless regularly paid and effectively commanded, might well have begun to live off the land as did many troops in Sierra Leone in the past.

Finally, a British withdrawal after a comprehensive military victory over the RUF would tip the balance of military power and risk restarting the war, as demonstrated by the aftermath of the withdrawal of Executive Outcomes in 1997. All the problems which helped create the war in the first place remained aggravated by the events of the past ten years. Such was obvious despite Whitehall denials that British involvement in logistics and training needed to continue for a long time. Habits of ill-discipline and corruption are endemic in the Sierra Leone armed forces, and many of the same soldiers are being recycled into the system.

Familiar problems – especially 'lost' wages and rations – are re-emerging as soldiers are placed under Sierra Leone command following their UK training. To reorient the SLA, the latter needed to ensure it was being effectively led. For that to happen, British officers must be placed in the chain of command, probably as deep as the rank of major. That step, while deemed to be essential by British officers on the ground, is politically risky for a Labour government already accused of 'mission creep' by its political opponents. It would also create unprecedented dependence by an African country on a former colonial power. The necessity for outside commitment to Sierra Leone goes further than the military sphere. In effect, a military option alone is doomed to failure in the sense that it cannot by itself stabilise Sierra Leone and could cause serious military repercussions throughout West Africa and further destabilising a troubled region. A military option, while necessary, can only achieve stability if it is part of a medium-term political strategy.

3.16.   CONCLUSION

As of 1999, of the country's estimated population of 4.7 million people, more than half (2.6 million) were either internally displaced or had become refugees in neighbouring states. Even though the causes of the conflict did show institutional breakdown and widespread neglect, Sankoh and his associates chose to exploit those genuine concerns by criminality, torture, drugs, plunder, and rape in battle (Chege 2002). The RUF distinguished themselves in war with forced conscription of adolescent boys; sexual enslavement of girls; shocking human mutilations; and wholesale destruction of settlements, schools, and government buildings. In fact, Chege's writing in 2002 noted that three years after the conflict, nobody knows with any certainty the total number of war casualties. A conservative estimate is 70,000, with hundreds of thousands of amputees and maimed people. The situation in Sierra Leone today (2008) is totally different from that reality such that it would be wrong to write that the international community and institutions totally failed in resolving the conflict in Sierra Leone.

4

METHODOLOGY

4.1. INTRODUCTION TO RESEARCH METHODOLOGICAL APPROACH

This chapter discusses the research design used for the study, including the methods used for analysis of the data. It draws on my experience of being a Sierra Leonean and doing a field research in the country. The work discusses physical risks both visible and invisible that were encountered during the fieldwork. The chapter also discusses other issues I encountered while conducting the research, specifically with regards to ethics, the relevance of informed consent, and issues such as describing the research and following strategies necessary to gain access to subjects.

A further challenge was to develop an approach that could provide detailed feedback and guidance and test its feasibility for implementation, whilst being mindful of views of community people and those of the international community. To address this, a two-stage methodological approach consisting of qualitative fieldwork—conducting in-depth interviews and group discussions and a small scale survey—was used.

4.2   RELEVANCE OF THE STUDY

Post-conflict reconstruction is a crucial part of a peace process as the fundamental pillars of society such as the rule of law and security are being (re)constructed during this phase, laying the foundation for state capacities which were non- or hardly existent during the conflict. Post-conflict reconstruction, thereby, also contributes to the transformation of a collapsed state to a failing state in the aftermath of a civil war. The context of a failed state for post-conflict reconstruction is highly significant for the field of conflict resolution as civil war activities go along with an increasing difficulty of the state to govern its territory and execute its governmental functions up to the collapse of state institutions. Conflicts are not to be isolated from their context, including state capacities, asymmetry of power relations, involvement of third parties, and so on. They cannot be analyzed appropriately if treated separately from the given environment and situation. Furthermore, the more challenging a conflict environment is, the more difficult is the successful implementation of post-conflict reconstruction. Thus, the study contributes to the understanding of the challenges posed to post-conflict reconstruction in the context of a failed state.

The peace process in Sierra Leone takes up the empirical part of the study. The Sierra Leonean civil war and its peace process have not received as much scholarly and media attention as, for instance, the civil wars in Rwanda and Bosnia. The literature on Sierra Leone focuses mainly on the political economy of the conflict and the military intervention of third parties, and neglects the evaluation of the post-conflict reconstruction process. The aim of the study is to convey a fieldwork and survey in Sierra Leone to gather first-hand data on the post-conflict reconstruction process and, based upon the gathered results, to draw up conclusions and recommendations for policymakers for future post-conflict reconstruction efforts in the context of a failed state.

4.3. GEOGRAPHICAL AREAS OF RESEARCH INTEREST

The research areas of interest included communities in the Bombali, Tonkolili, Port Loko and Kambia districts, all in Northern Sierra Leone, which had been severely devastated by the war. The basis for the selection of these geographic locations was mainly because most of the rural settlements, encompassing private housing, schools, health posts and significantly the social fabrics in the rural communities and elsewhere, were seriously destroyed beyond comprehension. During the ten years conflict, the vast majority of the mutineers hailed from the rural communities in Northern Sierra Leone. Of significant importance is that the region of interest contains the Temne people, the tribe of the late rebel leader, Col. Foday Saybana Sankoh. It also shares a boundary with neighbouring Guinea, a causative agent of a potential spill-over as a transit point for rebel groups into Guinea, Liberia and the Ivory Coast. This also makes it a linchpin in any research that attempts to understand and hopes to contribute to the stability of the sub-region. In my meetings with communities, I endeavoured to find out first what their understanding of the conflict were and then to seek to juxtapose that with that of donor agencies, especially DfID and its Community Reintegration Programme. I also gathered evidence on community perceptions, people's attitudes, expectations and experiences, tracing where those overlap with the reconstruction and nation building programmes being implemented in the region.

4.4.   QUALITATIVE FIELDWORK

The methods employed in this research were qualitative in nature. This approach was adopted to allow for individuals' views and experiences to be explored in detail. Qualitative methods neither seek, nor allow data to be given on the numbers of people holding a particular view nor having a particular set of experiences. The significance of qualitative research is to define and describe the range of emergent issues and explore linkages, rather than to measure their extent.

4.4.1.   SCHEME OF INTERVIEWS AND GROUPS

Due to the sensitivity of conflict issues within the various communities that suffered greatly or played a major role in the civil war and owing to the fact that the majority of people in the selected area were illiterates, face-to-face interviews of representative communities and strategic

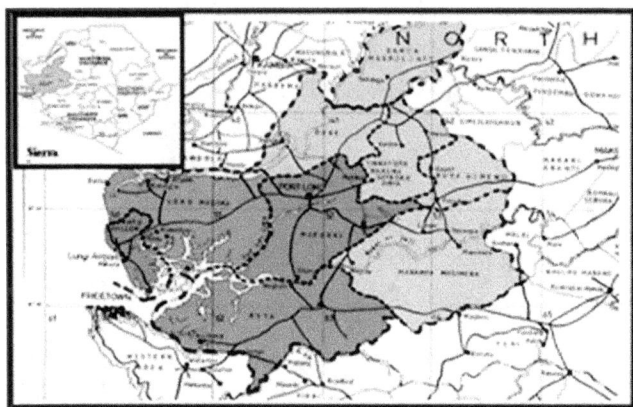

Fig. 1. Selected chiefdoms for the research project are shown coloured. The grey areas are those areas within Port Loko District that were still in rebel hands at the time of filing.

organisations in the northern and western parts of Sierra Leone (Figure 1) were conducted in most cases.

In order to accommodate some of the interviewees' limited literal level in exceptional cases, face-to-face interviews were considered to make it easier to breakdown the interview question in simpler terms for the understanding of the participants without losing the real sense of the question. This approach was economically viable in terms of both cost and time management. In some cases the survey was conducted via questionnaires.

4.4.2. CONDUCT OF INTERVIEWS AND GROUP DISCUSSIONS

In-depth interviews and group discussions were used via non-directive techniques. Each interview and group discussion was exploratory in form so that questioning could be responsive to the experiences and circumstances of the individuals involved. The question structure, which listed the key themes and sub topics to be addressed and the specific issues for coverage within each context, were based on a topic guide. The following demonstrates the main interview questions presented in an interview-friendly atmosphere to convey the following structures:

1. Whose idea was the programme in the first place - of your organisation or community?

2. What are the assumptions underpinning the design?

3. What was the motivation for your organisation or original interest in the project?

4. To what extent does the design of the programme relate to your organisation's wider objectives?

5. What was the process before they committed funds to the programme?

6. What was given as a justification for their intervention?

7. What was the objective of your programme as designed in the long frame (goal and purpose)?

8. How was the target group defined and what was this based on?

9. What other options were considered and rejected, and why?

10.   Does the project have a holistic focus: Is this focus on the previously marginalised, certain ethnic group victims of the war or its perpetrators?

11.   Is the project in Sierra Leone a unique one or a continuation of a project developed elsewhere?

4.5   CONTENT ANALYSIS OF REPRESENTATIVE TRANSCRIPTS

To extract the emergent evaluative impressions and themes, a Content Analysis—a scholarly methodology used by researchers in the social sciences to analyse recorded transcripts of interviews with participants—was performed on the coded data. Neuendorf (2002) defined Content Analysis in the context of an in-depth analysis employing quantitative or qualitative techniques of information or messages using a scientific method with attention to objective-intersubjectivity, a priori design, reliability, validity, replicability, and the like.

According to Krippendorff (2004), six major questions must be addressed:

1.   Which data are analysed?

2.   How are they defined?

3.   What is the population from which they are drawn?

4.   What is the context relative to which the data are analysed?

5.   What are the boundaries of the analysis?

6.   What is the target of the inferences?

In terms of the interview protocol adopted, the questions were derived from the aims and objectives and research questions of the study. The questions were structured to capture the subjective perceptions of respondents and or interviewees' experiential insights of the dynamics of the Sierra Leone civil war. Over all, 40 transcripts were representative for analysis. And of the interview questions, 11 questions that correlate to the main research questions and objectives were coded for analysis (Table 2). This was to ensure that a tidy analysis that matches the interview protocol format can be obtained. The type of content analytic strategy executed was a combination of both manifest and latent content analysis, as described by Gottschalk (1995). Manifest content is the visible or apparent elements of the responses, such as the particular phrases or words used by the participants, as well as the manner and the number of times they were used. Further, to grasp the meaning of particular words or phrases as used by a particular respondent or interviewee, I turn to latent content analysis which seeks to unravel the underlying aspects of the information or message interpretively. For example, in the questionnaire or interview data used in this report, words such as "corruption", "nepotism", "unemployment" and "mismanagement" were interpreted as negative mental impressions. Some qualitative research authors refer to this combination as thematic analysis (e.g. Gottschalk, 1995; Smith et al., 1992).

Table 2: Statistics

Questions	Valid	Missing
What were the underlying causes of the war?	40	0
What were the immediate causes of the war – what sparked it off?	40	0
Why did some people join the fighting?	40	0
Why did some people NOT join the fighting?	40	0
To what extent was ethnicity an issue in the origin and the implementation of the war?	40	0
What were the perceptions of community and political participation before, during and since the war?	40	0
To what extent did the CRP engage with the communities that it was trying to assist?	40	0
Has the DfID/CRP improved the opportunities for the vulnerable?	40	0
What were the objectives of the post war reconstruction project?	40	0
Did the project design facilitate these objectives being achieved?	40	0
What lessons have been learned?	40	0

Results

Table 3: Causative agents of the civil war

What were the underlying causes of the war?

		Frequency	Percent	Valid Percent	Cumulative Percent
Valid	Effects of colonization	10	25.0	25.0	25.0
	Hopelessness about future	19	47.5	47.5	72.5
	Corruptions and non-accountability	11	27.5	27.5	100.0
	Total	40	100.0	100.0	

Table 3 shows the various categories that were created to capture the responses. The categories were firmly grounded in the data. This was carefully done through a spiral process of expansion, merger and re-categorisation.

As shown in Table 3 above, responses show that interviewees or respondents' were given the benefit to state what they thought were the main causative agents of the war. The histogram below (Figure 2) shows that hopelessness about the future was a major agent of the war.

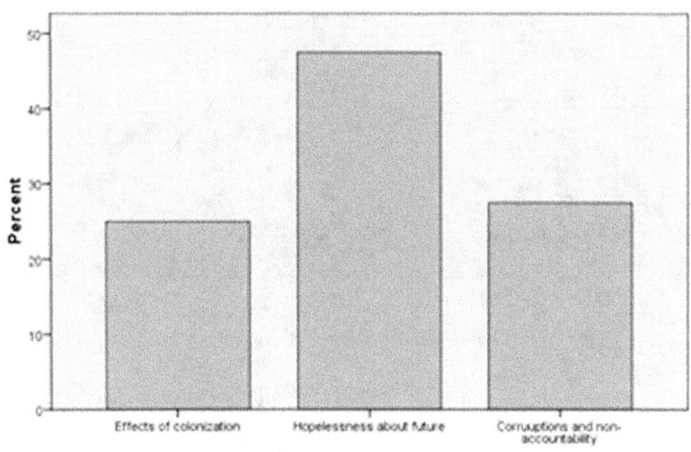

What were the underlying causes of the war?

Figure 2: Histogram of causative agents of the war

Table 4: Stimulus for the war

What were the immediate causes of the war – what sparked it off?

		Frequency	Percent	Valid Percent	Cumulative Percent
Valid	Party military e.g. Siaka Steven's APC	14	35.0	35.0	35.0
	Unemployment	18	45.0	45.0	80.0
	Not caring for and paying the military	8	20.0	20.0	100.0
	Total	40	100.0	100.0	

When questioned about stimulus for the immediate causes of the war, 45% of the interviewees strongly believe that the high level of employment in Sierra Leone can not be isolated (Figure 3).

What were the immediate causes of the war – what sparked it off?

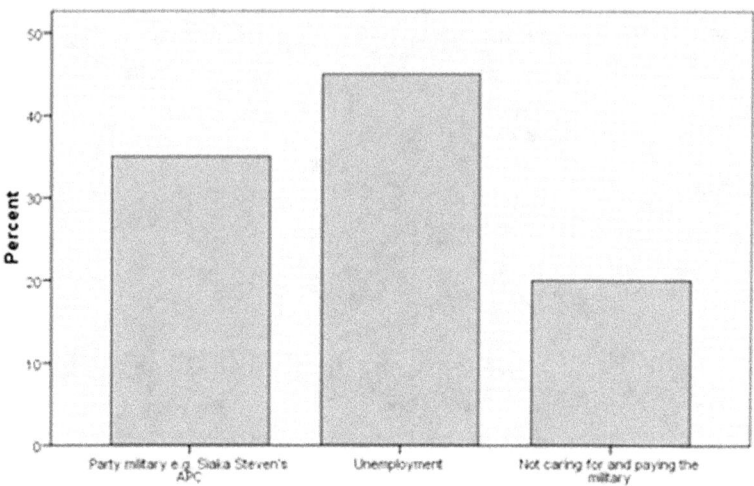

What were the immediate causes of the war – what sparked it off?

Figure 3 Histogram for stimulus of the war

To further exemplify, below are *in vivo* extracts from some of the 45% of interviewees:

"Unemployment and a lack of opportunity"
"Unemployment and lack of opportunity"

Table 5: Stimulus for joining in the fight

Why did some people join the fighting?

		Frequency	Percent	Valid Percent	Cumulative Percent
Valid	To amass wealth	12	30.0	30.0	30.0
	Faith in God	15	37.5	37.5	67.5
	Baseless RUF	13	32.5	32.5	100.0
	Total	40	100.0	100.0	

As shown in both Table 5 and Figure 4, faith played a major role in recruiting for the war. One particular in vivo response vividly captures this remarkable stimulus, as presented below:

"The faith I have in God"

Why did some people join the fighting?

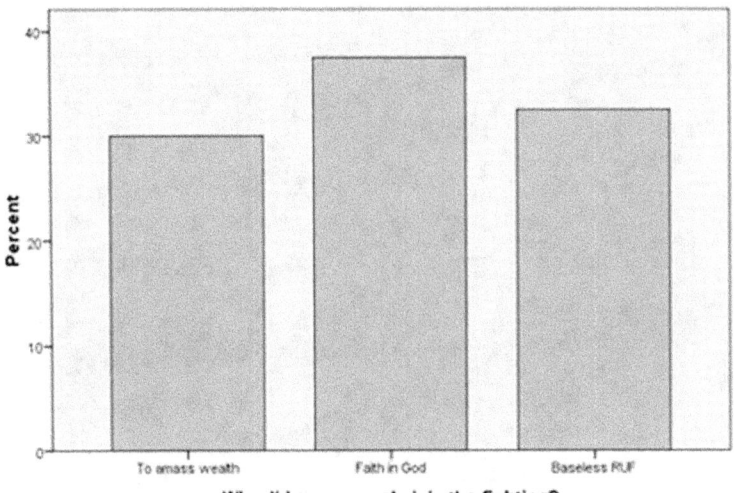

Figure 4 Stimulus for joining in the fight

The above histogram is reminiscent of a mental state about the factors that influence one to join the fighters during the civil war.

Table 6: Needless to join the fighting

Why did some people NOT join the fighting?

		Frequency	Percent	Valid Percent	Cumulative Percent
Valid	Proponent of peace	11	27.5	27.5	27.5
	War is stupid	18	45.0	45.0	72.5
	Worried about their life and safety	11	27.5	27.5	100.0
	Total	40	100.0	100.0	

While a fair balanced proportion was of the split opinion (Figure 5) that peace and security were necessary recipes for stability and therefore it would be good not to join the fighting, 45% of the participants thought it was a stupid idea to actually join the fighting. When asked, one interviewee answered as follows:

"*I fight my own war…Stupid to fight some ones war*"

Why did some people NOT join the fighting?

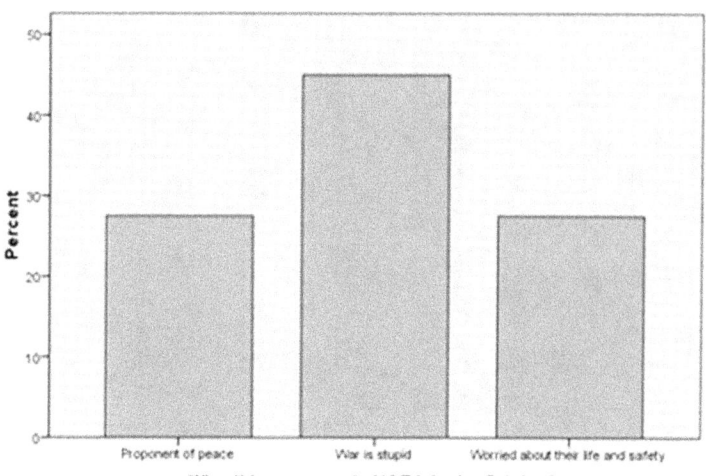

Why did some people NOT join the fighting?

Figure 5 Histogram representing opinions on not joining the fight.

Table 7: The role of ethnicity in the war

To what extent was ethnicity an issue in the origin and the implementation of the war?

		Frequency	Percent	Valid Percent	Cumulative Percent
Valid	Not at all	9	22.5	22.5	22.5
	A little bit	19	47.5	47.5	70.0
	Very much	12	30.0	30.0	100.0
	Total	40	100.0	100.0	

The role of ethnicity in the war presents mixed opinion as demonstrated in Table 7 and Figure 6, and exemplified in the following *in vivo* extracts:

"*Yes it was used by some to push their agenda forward*"

"No but it was use after the election…Yes it did, for instance the Kamajors in the South and the Gbethies in the North"
"Ethnicity became an issue with the election of 1996. Before that, it was between bad and good"
"To a lesser extent"
"Ethnicity was not one of the causes of the war…Ethniccity did not prolong the war in Sierra Leone"

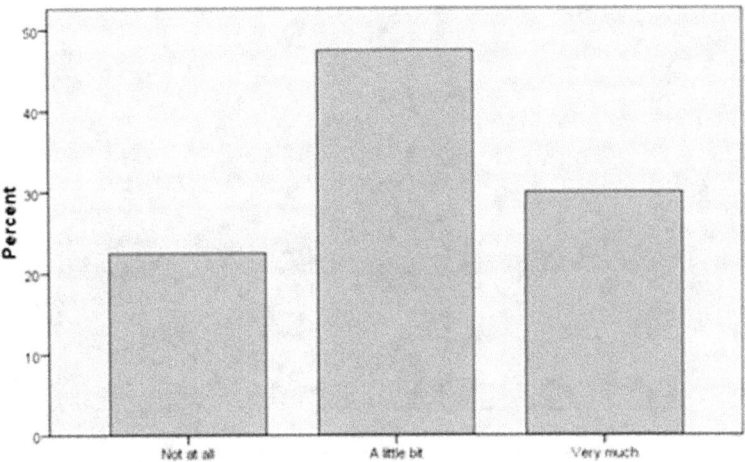

To what extent was ethnicity an issue in the origin and the implementation of the war?

Figure 6 The ethnic factor of the war

Table 8: Community perceptions

What were the perceptions of community and political participation before, during and since the war?

		Frequency	Percent	Valid Percent	Cumulative Percent
Valid	Peaceful co-existence	9	22.5	22.5	22.5
	Despondency	13	32.5	32.5	55.0
	Limited participation	11	27.5	27.5	82.5
	Positively	7	17.5	17.5	100.0
	Total	40	100.0	100.0	

An interesting indication manifested in responses with respect to the perceptions of community and political participations reveal a nearly fair balance as demonstrated by Table 8 and histogram below. One *in vivo* response is quoted as follows:

"The perception of communities in terms of Political participation before and during the war, was one of political apathy, and after the war, saw active political participation"

What were the perceptions of community and political participation before, during and since the war?

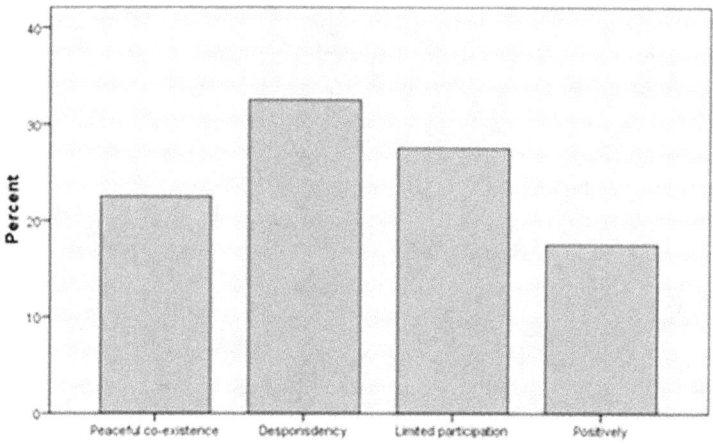

What were the perceptions of community and political participation before, during and since the war?

Figure 7 Community perceptions of the dynamics of conflict

Table 9: The CRP stimulus

To what extent did the CRP engage with the communities that it was trying to assist?

		Frequency	Percent	Valid Percent	Cumulative Percent
Valid	Don't know	11	27.5	27.5	27.5
	Focus group discussions	10	25.0	25.0	52.5
	Youth Groups	10	25.0	25.0	77.5
	Community consultation	9	22.5	22.5	100.0
	Total	40	100.0	100.0	

The bar chart (Figure 8) and Table 9 show clearer diagrammatic and numerical views of participants with regards to the extent of CRP's engagement with communities. One enthusiast's in vivo quote is as follows:

"It changed communities positively"

To what extent did the CRP engage with the communities that it was trying to assist?

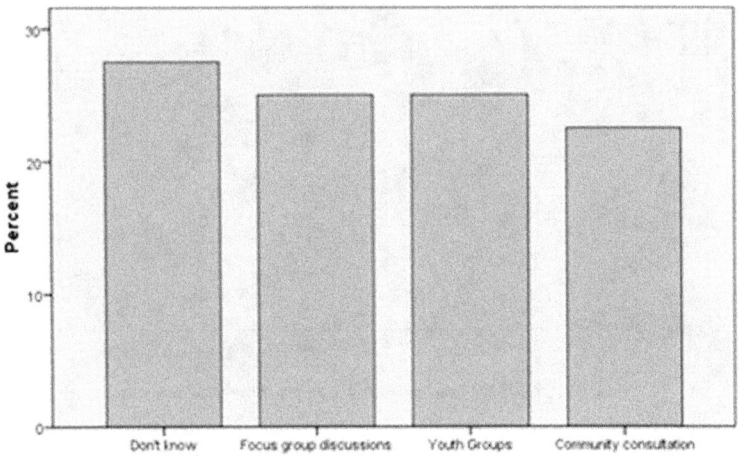

To what extent did the CRP engage with the communities that it was trying to assist?

Figure 8 The CRP stimulus and communities

Table 10: Improved DfID/CRP opportunities

Has the DfID/CRP improved the opportunities for the vulnerable?

		Frequency	Percent	Valid Percent	Cumulative Percent
Valid	Care for the wounded and displaced	15	37.5	37.5	37.5
	Resettlement	15	37.5	37.5	75.0
	Absolutely none	10	25.0	25.0	100.0
	Total	40	100.0	100.0	

The statistics shown in Table 10 is cleared painted graphically in Figure 9 below in terms of whether DfID/CRP improved opportunities for the vulnerable. One interviewee's *in vivo* is presented as follows:

"The people of Sierra Leone but most importantly the youth. There is no hope for them"

Has the DfID/CRP improved the opportunities for the vulnerable?

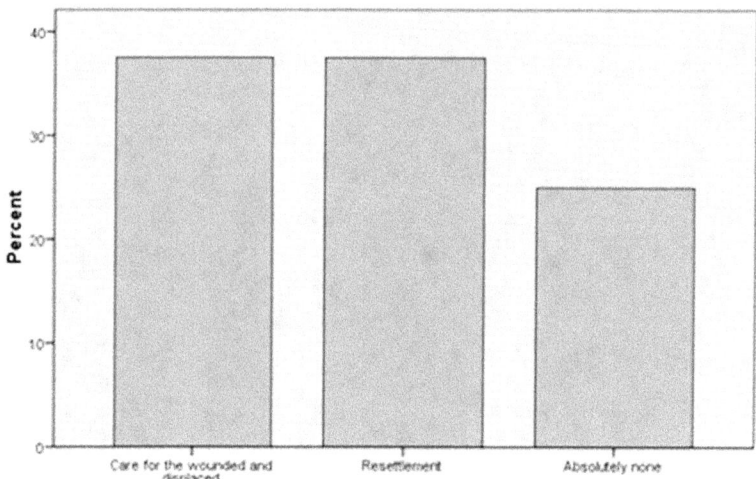

Has the DfID/CRP improved the opportunities for the vulnerable?

Figure 9 DfID/CRP improved opportunities

Table 11: Objectives of post war reconstruction

What were the objectives of the post war reconstruction project?

		Frequency	Percent	Valid Percent	Cumulative Percent
Valid	To address the past	9	22.5	22.5	22.5
	To create home and opportunities	18	45.0	45.0	67.5
	3	13	32.5	32.5	100.0
	Total	40	100.0	100.0	

Majority of the participants attempted to response to this question as objectives as possible, 45% interviews concurring that the main objects of post-war reconstruction to evolve opportunities for survival. Below are three *in vivo* extracts:

"Address the cause of the conflict"

"To create hope and opportunities for the people of Sierra Leone"

"To address the grievances of the past"

What were the objectives of the post war reconstruction project?

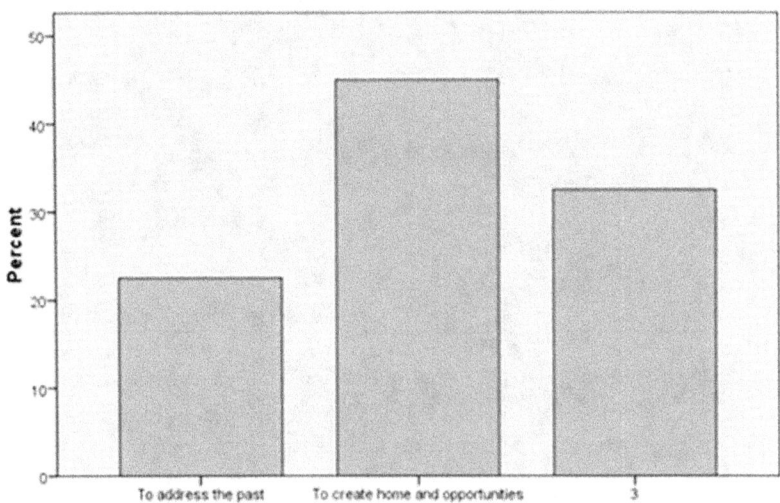

What were the objectives of the post war reconstruction project?

Figure 10 Post war reconstruction

Table 12: Project design versus objectives

Did the project design facilitate these objectives being achieved?

		Frequency	Percent	Valid Percent	Cumulative Percent
Valid	No	13	32.5	32.5	32.5
	Yes	27	67.5	67.5	100.0
	Total	40	100.0	100.0	

With regards to the graphic representation of Table 12 and respective figure 11 based on the subject-matter, below are *in vivo* extracts:

"Yes"

"No, what it did then was to address the effects of the war and not the underlying issues which go all the way to the West"

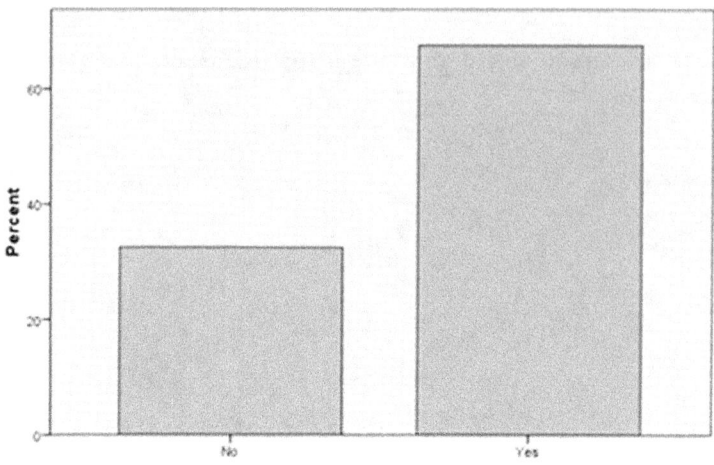

Did the project design facilitate these objectives being achieved?

Figure 11 Project design versus objectives

Table 13: Lessons learned

What lessons have been learned?

		Frequency	Percent	Valid Percent	Cumulative Percent
Valid	Naive to align with incumbent	11	27.5	27.5	27.5
	Peace is a decision	6	15.0	15.0	42.5
	Community consultation is roadmap	16	40.0	40.0	82.5
	Roads and bridges don't solve conflicts	7	17.5	17.5	100.0
	Total	40	100.0	100.0	

The participants presented diverse views on the lesson learned as demonstrated in Table 13 and Figure 12, and also in the sample *in vivo* extracts:

"Democracy is a very expensive luxury and in a post war situation, democracy may not be the best idea"

"They cannot solve the conflict by building road and bridges. Trade restriction and issues like debt has for more reaching effect African states than post war programmes"

"At post war, it is naive to align with the incumbent since they may be the cause of the conflict"

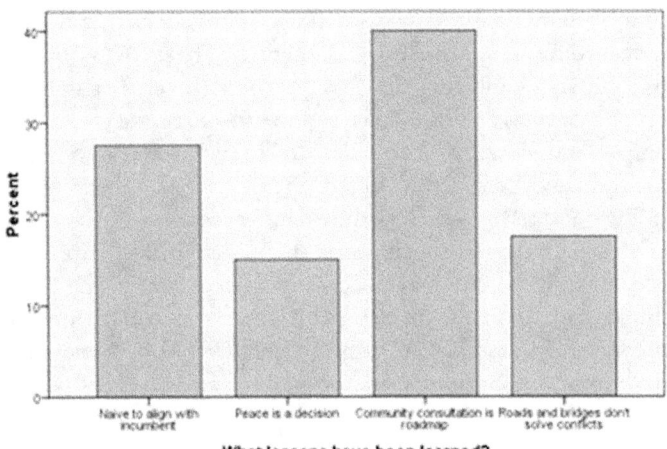

Figure 12 Lessons learned

Executive Summary

From the content analysis presented above a number of notable indicators from the emergent themes are positive and constructive. These indicators can seriously be taken to show the impact and potential of such fieldwork in war-torn environs. The analysis unravelled a potentially relevant and productive area of lessons learned that reveals development of ideal framework for reconstruction programmes.

4.6. THE ANALYSIS OF QUALITATIVE MATERIAL USING MATRIX MAPPING

Material collected through qualitative methods is invariably unstructured and unwieldy. Much of it is textural, consisting of verbatim transcriptions of interviews and discussions. Moreover, the internal content of the material is usually detailed and in micro-form (for example, accounts of experiences and inarticulate explanations). The primary aim of any analytical method is to provide a means of exploring coherence and structure within a cumbersome data set whilst retaining a hold on the original accounts and observations from which it is derived.

Qualitative analysis is essentially about detection and exploration of the data, deriving sense of the data by looking for coherence and structure within the data. Matrix Mapping works from verbatim transcripts and involves a systematic process of sifting, summarising and sorting the material according to key issues and themes. The process begins with a familiarisation stage and includes a researcher's review of the transcripts. Based on the coverage of the topic guide, the researchers' experiences of conducting the fieldwork and their preliminary review of the data, a thematic framework is constructed. The analysis then proceeds by summarising and synthesising the data according to this thematic framework using a range of techniques such as cognitive mapping and data matrices. When all the data have been sifted according to the core themes, the analyst begins to map the data and identify features within the data: defining concepts, mapping the range and nature of phenomenon, creating typologies, finding associations, and providing explanations.

The analyst reviews the summarised data; compares and contrasts the perceptions, accounts, or experiences; searches for patterns or connections within the data and seeks explanations internally within the data set. Piecing together the overall picture is not simply aggregating patterns. It also involves a process of weighing up the salience and dynamics of issues, and searching for structures within the data that have explanatory power, rather than simply seeking a multiplicity of evidence. This report is mainly based on the themes and issues arising from the analysis of the qualitative data from the interviews and group discussions.

4.7.   SURVEY SAMPLE

Respondents for interview were determined on the basis of their involvement and experience during and after the war. The key subject areas and issues within which questioning took place included understanding the causes of the conflict and lessons learned from it; the reconstruction programme, its design and delivery, performance, sustainability issues; role of external agents, local dominant groups and ordinary people in the rebuilding process.

In particular, interviews were conducted within a broad sect of society, with chiefs, village elders, councillors, victims, perpetrators, religious leaders, health, education, police, arm force personnel, staff of local and international NGOs, government ministries or departments, civil society, etc. In essence, this sample was prompted by my personal experience and with others by recommendations from community elders and DfID staff.

4.7.1.   CONDUCT OF SURVEY

Potential respondents were sent electronic or hard format invitation letters as same for the depth/focus group respondents. The extension of invitation was followed up by email including the draft guidance and a short information sheet. Respondents were sent a reminder two days before the deadline, and those who had not completed the questionnaire after this deadline were called and extension given for them to complete it.

A crucial part of a good research design concerns making sure that it addresses the needs of the research. To put this in another way, somehow we need to ensure that the questions asked were the right ones. It is also important to avoid the problem of having inadequate data and inadequate inferences from the data that the method of analysis is known, and it should inform the preceding stages of the research.

As such, researchers are advised in all cases to start their research by setting down the aims for the research, the hypothesis and its objectives, to review the relevant literature and also some preliminary research which in my case was done amongst colleagues at the Graduate School and with NGOs in Sierra Leone. It was based on fulfilling the above aims that my interview schedule was designed and questions selected for the field work.

4.7.2.   SURVEY QUESTIONS

Questions raised were phrased towards providing answers to the associated risks of state failure, and associated structural or root causes of conflict and violence. Since the research was conducted within the North of Sierra Leone and within the confines of the DfID Community Reintegration Programme, the research examines the peace-building mechanisms being developed there and implemented vis-à-vis conflict prevention and mediation. Most important is its holistic approach to addressing the root causes. It assesses how holistic those approaches are?

One of the major components is to question whether they addressed the root causes or if the process of supporting post-war reconstruction after civil war reinforces the old structures and continue to marginalize the poor. Or do they provide the opportunity for the previously marginalized to be integrated into the decision-making process and to establish a better future? With the benefit of hindsight, did the process of reintegration adopted by the CRP recognise and address the root causes of the war and provide an opportunity to rebuild communities in which all could benefit – including the previously marginalized? If not, did this reflect the way the project was planned or the way that it was implemented?

4.7.3.   RESPONSES TO THE SURVEY

From the sample of 400 individuals, 50 responses to the survey were received (interviewed or questionnaire). Although this was a small number of responses, it was relatively representative of the overall targeted sample population. It was also imperative that a distinction between the roles and those of other players engaged in the reconstruction process could be drawn. Before the interview, I first selected 1 young male, 2 middle-aged males, and one older male all of high socio-economic status, and continued until all the boxes were completed. A sample of 50 is used, with male and female sections evenly matched. Interviews were only undertaken with persons who fitted these categories. In total, 50 people were interviewed, which excluded members of the communities as follows:

Table 14: Selection Method

		GENDER								
		MALES			1Sub-1Total	FEMALES			1Sub 1Tot	1Total
Age		15/20	21/45	46+		15/20	21/45	46+		
Socio-Economic Status	High	1	2	1	4	1	2	1	4	8
	Middle	1	6	2	9	1	6	2	9	18
	Low	2	7	3	12	2	7	3	12	24
					25				25	50

Table 14 illustrates the selection method involved in the selection process used for the interview. A sample of 50, with male and female sections matched to represent the total population of the community.

4.7.4. ANALYSIS OF THE SURVEY DATA

The data from the survey was entered into an Excel spreadsheet developed for this research. It was then analysed by producing pivot tables to give cross tabulations of answers to questions by organisation type. The data from the open ended questions was analysed by putting comments into a matrix, and looking for commonalities and differences between answer types.

4.8. THE USE OF QUANTITATIVE DATA IN THIS REPORT

Graphs showing responses to the survey questions have been omitted and replaced by qualitative responses. Data from the open ended questions in the survey are included alongside the qualitative data, and are identified as being survey answers.

4.9. CHALLENGES FACED DURING THE RESEARCH

There were several challenges faced by the research team in the undertaking of this research, each of which is outlined below, together with recommendations for future research of a similar nature.

4.9.1. ETHICAL CHALLENGES

Since the research was dealing with communities and addressing human behavioural patterns, ethical considerations, especially confidentiality and informed consent were carefully handled. It requires me not to disclose transcript of an interview if its sensitivity would bring undue harm to the interviewee or when he or she wishes me not to do so. Berg defines informed consent as the knowing consent of individuals to participate in an exercise of their choice, free from any element of fraud, deceit, duress, or similar unfair inducement or manipulation (Berg 2009). To establish trust and appear unbiased, my approach was to listen carefully and not to offer any personal views. I sought to develop rapport, knowing when to probe and prompt.

The building of trust is a developmental task as trust is not something that suddenly appears after certain matters have been accomplished. But it is something to be worked on. Trust is not established once and for all. It is fragile. Even trust that has taken long time to build can be destroyed overnight in the face of an ill-advised action. Techniques learned at the Graduate School serve as a reference; coupled with continuous supervision with my supervisor and lessons learned from a pilot project I made with colleagues at the Graduate School served as an invaluable resource during my research trip.

4.9.2.   INFORMED CONSENT

Bearing in mind the fragility of the Sierra Leonean with the situation as regards the Truth and Reconciliation Commission (TRC) and the Special Court (SC) to try perpetrators of the near-ten year civil war, it was apparent that gaining *informed consent* was going to be a difficult task. However, as Eisner notes, "As researchers, we must find an acceptable balance (to whom) between our rights as researchers and the right of participants to self determination, privacy and dignity" (Eisner 1991). In view of the prevailing circumstance, I applied *the twin principle of confidentiality and informed consent*. Confidentiality in this context means that people know that some of the colleagues were interviewed but do not know what was said, whilst anonymous means that people did not know that some of them were interviewed. These scenarios compare with ballot casting—For instance, when one votes in an election how one voted is confidential but one is not necessarily anonymous - i.e. it is known that they voted. Within a village people may see that I am interviewing specific people (i.e. it is not anonymous) but will not know what they say (i.e. it is confidential).

4.9.3.   RAISING EXPECTATIONS

Hypothetically, reintegration programmes tend to re-enforce old social structures and do not provide an opportunity for the marginalized. In probing communities about such issues of opportunity and marginalisation, I was mistaken for an aid worker. I therefore sought to clarify my purpose, to avoid raising such expectations.

4.9.4.   RE-OPENING OLD WOUNDS

The dirty war tactics that were employed in the conflict left a legacy of being one of the most vicious of civil wars in the world. As such, probing into these areas was dealt with exercising great sensitivity and caution to avoid re-opening old wounds of subjects questioned, especially on issues they did not wish to respond to or which they deemed provocative. It is obvious that re-living distressing and painful experiences may be a very potent experience and could cause long-term psychological distress. To prevent me from causing this or inadvertently probing into these areas that respondents did not wish to talk about, I employed restraint and also tried to know when to stop. Being a native of that country offered me with broader knowledge of the cultural characteristics which also helped.

4.9.5.   SECURITY RISKS

A lack of knowledge of what could go wrong during fieldwork can be frustrating to the researcher as a person and to the project. As mentioned earlier, there is partial truth in the idea of safety because of researcher 'familiarity' with terrain or environment (Griffiths 1998: 361). Familiarity is not necessarily a guarantee of safety because of unpredictable events stemming from suspicion, change of political climate and traditional/cultural conservatism.

As such, safety was a fundamental issue of this research for both communities and me. Even though I was familiar with the environment and know that there was relative peace, the Special Court and the Truth and Reconciliation Commission unintentionally heightened tensions in Sierra Leone. Thus, identifying certain individuals as victims had the potential of putting them in danger, whilst involving the community in some of the circumstances did resemble investigating financial dealings of non-governmental organizations. Bringing communities together for discussion, especially ex-combatants may inadvertently be putting them at risk. On the contrary, these potential limitations did not in any away divert the substance of this work.

4.10   RECOMMENDATIONS

This section discusses views of members of the international community and that of community people and identifies the recommendations which were felt to be most important.

4.10.1.   LONG-TERM PLANNING

The first recommendation relates to the fact that the study was conducted over a six month period (December 2004 – May 2005), producing a snapshot of persons and organisations involved in the reconstruction process during that particular period. It is possible that the views of the post war community, including those that were affected by the war, may have changed over time. Further, there is also problem with the representative population studied. Although I spared no means to inform victims about the study, the response rate was relatively low. Participation was entirely voluntary, possibly resulting in a selection bias which may have influenced the findings of the study.

4.10.2. LEVEL OF ENGAGEMENT

The second limitation has to do with the extent to which the findings can be generalized beyond the cases studied. The number of cases is too limited for broad generalizations.

4.10.3. TRUST AND RESPECT (RECOMMENDATION 1)

Trust and respect was also identified as a key recommendation and was understood to link closely to other recommendations such as long term planning (rec 1) and levels of engagement and power (rec 2). Honesty and truth were felt to be key factors in building trust and respect with communities. They provide an effective premise for community engagement. To further exemplify, below is *in vivo* quote of an interviewee:

> *"...I think if you're trying to engage any kind of community at any level you must attain high trust and respect from that community. Without that, no intervention that you try to get into the community will work. So I think that's paramount really in terms of engaging communities."*

4.10.4. TRAINING (RECOMMENDATION 2)

Training and an understanding of the history of the causes of conflict for those working on the reconstruction programme was considered to be an important factor of the work, but it is also stressed that the resources need to be available for this training.

4.10.5. CULTURAL SHIFT (RECOMMENDATION 3)

This was a recommendation which respondents particularly felt they were already working towards. Arguably, most people who work within this remit are aware of the dangers and consequences of stereotyping, as stereotyping target groups can reduce the effectiveness of initiatives, resulting in set targets not being met. One particular *in vivo* text extract vividly captures this call, as presented below:

> *"My general experience is probably 80 maybe 90 percent of the people from the west who work in the reconstruction programmes in one way or another are usually fairly sensitive to the dangers of stereotyping, because they know that if they over-stereotype or they overdo the sort of target group recognition they won't be able to achieve their objectives."*

4.11. CONCLUSION

The work attempts to put into practice issues about access, ethics, security risk, politics and the researcher's role in the field. I have also indicated that the researcher as an 'insider' or 'outsider' has strengths and constraints. Thus, an advance familiarity with the field of research interest can in some ways threaten research work. For instance, an outsider's research interview questions can be construed as being invasive at all cost simply to extract information.

5

RESULTS AND REFLECTIONS

FIELD WORK RESULTS AND THEMATIC REFLECTIONS ON THE COLLECTED DATA

5.1.   INTRODUCTION

An understanding of the war and its root causes are important recipes for successful post-conflict reconstruction. Without such understanding, reconstruction efforts face the risk of failure (Bredel 2003). It is only after when the potential causative agents are identified will reconstruction stand a chance to address potential threats to the achievement of sustainable peace and stability.

With Sierra Leone in the frame, the general consensus from most literature is that it failed. This then raised the issue about what should be an adequate response of the international community to a post-conflict situation such as Sierra Leone that has left a failed or severely impeded state. Unlike other types of civil wars with limited international and regional ramifications, the issues surrounding failed states are very complex; leaving them alone or supporting one side may only contribute to exacerbating the conflict as demonstrated by the Sierra Leonean scenario.

5.2.   BACKGROUND TO THE DFID POST-CONFLICT RECONSTRUCTION PROGRAMME

With the resumption of conflict in Sierra Leone in 2000, DfID intervened in the post-war reconstruction phase in Sierra Leone directly and also indirectly through Agrisystems. A U.K. based NGO was asked to submit a design proposal for the rebuilding of Sierra Leone (DfID 2002). The context for the intervention was spelt out as follows: "With the support of the President of Sierra Leone, DfID has decided to make a direct intervention in order to assist in the implementation of the DDR programme. Ensuring that the reinvigoration of reintegration activities extends beyond ex-combatants and brings broader development benefits to communities in Sierra Leone" (DfID 2004).

The overarching objective of DfID is to underpin the promotion of sustainable peace, security and stability in Sierra Leone (Programme Goal) through the provision of livelihood opportunities. An effective programme is the key element of the British Government's overall strategy for achieving peace in Sierra Leone. It is also an essential component of DfID's current development strategy. This is heavily weighted towards assistance to the security sector and rebuilding a democratic process. In recognition of the fact that increased security will allow NGOs and other agencies to deliver humanitarian relief and provide a firmer foundation for longer-term development work which is needed if sustainable progress is to be made towards meeting the international development targets of democracy. The goals of the post war programmes were defined by DfID's idea but the design of the activities to achieve those outputs was undertaken by Agrisystems and the NGOs concerned.

Britain is the largest bilateral donor to Sierra Leone. The UK supports an extensive programme including reconstruction of war-damaged areas, reintegration of former combatants, training and strengthening of the police and armed forces, judicial reform and a wide-ranging programme of governance.

The UK government committed to a ten-year programme of support to the social and economic development of Sierra Leone. The agreement, known as a Poverty Reduction Framework Arrangement (PRFA), committed Britain to £120 million of support for development programmes. This funding is a combination of bilateral funds from the Department for International Development (DfID) budget and from the Africa Conflict Reduction Pool.

These were collectively funded and managed by DfID, the Foreign and Commonwealth Office (FCO) and the Ministry of Defence.

5.3.   DfID/COMMUNITY REINTEGRATION PROGRAMME (CRP)

The CRP is aiming to re-establish inclusive social, economic and cultural networks at community level in northern Sierra Leone. This is leading to reintegration of former combatants and other war-affected people into viable and stable communities. The CRP began in March 2001 and initially covered three Chiefdoms within Port Loko District. It has since been extended to forty-two Chiefdoms within the Districts of Bombali, Tonkolili, Kambia and Port Loko. Management of the CRP is contracted out to Agrisystems Limited, a consultancy specialising in post-conflict management.

The work involves understanding community needs, fostering reintegration and reconciliation, reviving agricultural production, supporting small-scale enterprise development, rehabilitating physical infrastructure and improving water, sanitation and health. The CRP has direct and indirect beneficiaries. It has worked directly to identify and cater for the priority needs of approximately 100,000 people in more than 200 communities. Indirectly, between 700,000 and 800,000 people are benefiting within the targeted Chiefdoms. Additionally, the CRP also assisted the work of the national Commission for Disarmament, Demobilisation and Reintegration (NCDDR) by providing vocational training programmes and toolkits for over 5,000 ex-combatants and unemployed youths. The 279 projects so far supported under the CRP have:

- Through women's groups and agricultural associations, provided seeds and tools to more than 12,000 rural families;

- Returned more than 7,000 acres of agricultural land to sustainable production;

- Supported more than 160 small businesses and associations through business skills training and the provision of grants for revolving credit;

- Constructed and rehabilitated five key road arteries including repairs to bridges, culverts and ferries (e.g. the Mabanta Ferry, in Port Loko District);

- Rehabilitated 15 schools;

- Built and rehabilitated civic structures, including 14 Police Stations, court barries, markets and a customs building;

- Supplied 20,000 families with clean, affordable water;

- Conducted 80 community-based health education and HIV/AIDS campaigns.

In addition to these works, the value-added component is significant. The Programme has helped to:

- Build capacity of implementing partners and local government, that will leave behind a core of national expertise able to design, implement and monitor community-based programmes;

- Promote reconciliation and unification through the funding and management of sporting and cultural events;

- Address environmental and production concerns through the establishment of community forest nurseries and community fisheries to offset the over-exploitation of scarce natural resources.

A total of £12.9 million was committed to the programme and it was finished in September 2003.

5.4.   DISARMAMENT AND DEMOBILISATION

By 15 May 2000, about 20,042 ex-combatants (XCs) were disarmed—4,949 of these were from the RUF, 10,055 from the Armed Forces Revolutionary Council (AFRC) and 9,038 from the Civil Defence Forces. About seven percent of these were children, and were put under the care of UNICEF rather than NCDDR. However, there were other challenges: when the Peace Accord was signed in 2001, about 40% of the country was in the hands of the Revolutionary United Front (RUF) who twice that year broke the ceasefire and destroyed the demobilization centres. As a result the United Nations had to suspend the demobilization in four of the seven centres.

Military sources recount that from 45,000 that were in the process of being demobilized and reintegrated, only a mere 6,000 was accounted for (Reuters, 27 July 2000). The demobilised child soldiers that were with UNICEF, with the breakdown, also went back to the RUF, thereby presenting a huge problem for the NCDDR to have to go through the whole process all over again. However, despite the problems associated with intimidation from some quarters of the RUF on those intending to disarm and a lack of funds, a renewed vigour was brought into the process with the timely arrival of the British Army. The United Nations Mission in Sierra Leone also in October 2000, called for a thorough overhaul of the programme (United Nations 2002), a speedy demobilization process (United Nations 2000) and the provision of incentives, which is seen as a vital prerequisite for reintegration.

Since the long-term plan of both DfID and the United Nations was to transform these disgruntled and malcontent elements, efforts were first and foremost put into extensive security sector reforms and in training and equipping about 8,500 of the former SLA forces. The shortage of funds which also led to a breakdown of the former accord was also saved with $1580 million from the international community and a further USD 306,094 to the Multi Donor Trust Fund (MDTF) by the Japanese government (IRIN, 30 November 2000). This yielded huge returns with eventual disarmament and demobilisation of almost 720 former combatants by January 2002 from all warring parties, including 4,751 women (6.5%) and 6,787children (9.4%), of which 506 were girls (DfID 2002).

From the outset, there was the recognition of the large presence of child soldiers (up to 50% of fighters in rebel forces were believed to be under 18) and women (estimates ranged between 10% and 30%) among the various forces. 42,330 weapons and 1.2 million pieces of ammunition were also collected and destroyed marking the official end of the civil war in Sierra Leone (Bundu 2001). On the other hand, the demobilised CDF ex-combatants returned to their communities, as they saw the process basically as involving disarmament and registration, without the need for encampment and resettlement faced by the RUF and the RSLA. Two factors posed a challenge to the fragile peace; first the continued close-knit connection of former RUF fighters and second, even though the RUF has been disarmed, demobilized, and metamorphosed into a formal – albeit unsuccessful – political party, yet like the CDF, former RUF combatants have not completely 'disappeared'. Some former RUF combatants have crossed into Liberia. While Liberia's civil war recently came to a close, the UN has yet to make its presence felt in much of the outlying areas of that country.

5.5.   COMMUNITY REINTEGRATION PROJECT (CRP)

CRP provided employment for ex-combatants and resettling internally displaced peoples while rebuilding essential infrastructure. The programme tested a number of approaches to the reintegration of XCs through reconciliation with Other War-Affected Persons (OWAPs), adopting a holistic approach in which both XCs and OWAPs could see a future for themselves through co-operation and through belief in a shared future. The pilot phase of the CRP has therefore delivered 31 projects in a range of fields including infrastructure, water and sanitation, shelter, small business development, livelihoods and social reintegration (DfID 2002).

5.6.   SECURITY SECTOR REFORM

Through the International Military Assistance and Training Team (IMATT), the Sierra Leone Army has been restructured and is undergoing a retraining programme. While the Sierra Leone Army is responsible for maintaining national security, the Police also have a key role to play in ensuring long-term security. During the war the Police were among the first targets of the rebel forces. DfID and UNAMSIL have provided support in the restructuring of the Sierra Leone Police through staff training and the development of the infrastructure. In preparation for the withdrawal of UNAMSIL in Sierra Leone which eventually took place in 2005.

The Special Court and the Truth and Reconciliation Commission were established to address issues of justice and reconciliation. The purpose of the Special Court was to bring to justice 'those bearing the greatest responsibility for war crimes committed since 1996'. The Court was created at the request of the Government of Sierra Leone, with the support of the international community through the UN. The Truth and Reconciliation Commission was established in 2002 to give a report on the causes of the war (including an historical narrative) and to offer a road-map with recommendations on a range of reforms necessary to prevent a new conflict. These include governance, corruption, management of the diamond mines and the national recovery plan.

An Infrastructure Reconstruction Programme (SLIRP)—provided support to the re-establishment of government services in newly accessible parts of the country by building or rehabilitating key infrastructures. A Law Development Project (LDP) was introduced to help restore and strengthen the legal institutional framework and update the legal code.

5.7.   GOVERNANCE REFORM

Admittedly, it is easier to measure the impact of large-scale reconstruction projects that rebuild physical infrastructure. Yet, reconstruction of the social fabric of Sierra Leonean society is equally important (Thomson 2007). Public goods such as 'justice' are subjective and open to varying interpretations, and therefore escape quantification. But, if any lesson is to be learned from Sierra Leone's civil war and the preceding decades of poor governance, it is that sources of political, economic, and social grievances cannot be ignored. Two essential legal prerequisites are needed in these, human rights and restructuring the judicial system in general. On the area of human rights, the confidence and security perception of people, including ex-combatants depend, to a large extent, on how past and present human rights are dealt with.

Judicial reform is necessary if people's desire for justice and reconciliation is to be met. There is a compelling need to bring the perpetrators of violence to justice if the current peace-building momentum is to be sustained. The United Kingdom's DfID and the IMATT, each have instituted several programmes aimed at ameliorating civil-military relations throughout Sierra Leone. The hybrid court set up by agreement between the government of Sierra Leone and the UN has been addressing serious violations of war crimes. However, because of its limited operational time, the court system at the district level needs to be revamped to bolster its effectiveness. Immediately after the conflict, there were no courts in the country outside the capital Freetown, and the Provincial cities of Bo and Kenema, thus making access to legal redress for most people in the North and East of the country impossible. Addressing the acute shortage of legal manpower should be a central component of any judicial reform. Bah for instance noted, "there are only 20 practising judges for the whole of Sierra Leone, most of whom sit only in Freetown with the two magistrates in Bo and Kenema the only exceptions. There are only about 100 lawyers within jurisdiction. Of this number; eight are in Bo and Kenema, while there are no practising lawyers in the Northern Province". Through the DfID temporary work programme, which I shall be dealing with later, courts were reconstructed and incentives put forth to encourage judges and police to go to the interior.

5.8.   ADDRESSING CORRUPTION

Government corruption and weak capacity were problems well before the civil war began (Grant 2002), thus, the simple act of holding "free and fair elections" should not be expected to solve these problems. If reconstruction plans were to be effective, it was considered especially by DfID that attention should be focused in addressing one of the leading causes of Sierra Leone's civil war: corruption. Not only are foreign donors wary of corruption, but so too – and perhaps most importantly for long-term reconstruction and sustainable economic growth – are foreign investors. Of course, eradicating corruption is easier said than done. Grant argued, nevertheless, that some relatively inexpensive though useful changes could be implemented for the short term, such as drastically improving transparency in government accounts and its awarding of contracts. To assist in this venture, the DfID suggested to the government to replace some of the top Sierra Leone civil servants with British civil servants to take Sierra Leone through the transition.

On 3 February 2000 the Sierra Leone Government moved further by enacting the Anti-Corruption Act. This paved the way for the founding of the Anti-Corruption Commission (ACC), which came into being on 1 January 2001 with the assistance of the United Kingdom's Department for International Development (DfID). The ACC is tasked to counter the ever-increasing corruption in Sierra Leone and will pay particular attention to corrupt payments to government officials and the misappropriation of public and donor funds. However, improving government capacity or eradicating corruption was no easy feat when the government was also implicated in the practice. It was therefore practical to discuss ways of reducing government corruption otherwise government ability to implement policy, enforce laws and regulations, and ensure that scarce funds reach those segments of the population in greatest need might be affected. Sierra Leone's present score is still low in terms of 'Anti-Corruption and Transparency' at 3.01 out of a possible 7 points. If the perception grows that corruption has decreased in Sierra Leone, then international and bilateral aid and lending agencies will have greater confidence in allocating assistance to the country.

5.9.   THE LAW AND JUDICIARY

Like Sierra Leone's other most basic institutions, the legal and penal system was destroyed in the war. The rebels targeted the police and prisons. Through the Law Reform Commission, DfID has funded the rehabilitation of courts, provided equipment and is helping to train personnel of the judicial department. The organisation has also helped to restore and strengthen the legal institutional framework, and updated the legal code. Two police training programmes (UN Civilian Police training through UNAMSIL, and the Commonwealth Police project) are supporting the recruitment and training of the police.

The legal system is based on English law and customary laws indigenous to local tribes. The judiciary comprises of the Supreme Court, Court of Appeal, High Court, and Magistrate Court. The Supreme and Appeal Courts sit only in Freetown. The High and Magistrate Courts sit in any of the districts. To date Sierra Leone has not accepted compulsory International Court of Justice (ICJ) jurisdiction.

5.10.   SPECIAL COURT

The SCSL was established to bring justice to those bearing the greatest responsibility for war crimes committed since 1996'. The Court was created at the request of the Government of Sierra Leone and supported by the international community. The work of the Prosecution team, under Chief Prosecutor, David Crane, began in July 2002. Twelve people have so far been indicted, including former Liberia President Charles Taylor, former Interior Minister San Hinga Norman, and former Member of Parliament (MP) Johnny Paul Koroma. Nine of the twelve indictees are presently in custody facing trials. Sam Bockarie, a key lieutenant of rebel leader Foday Sankoh was reported killed in Liberia shortly after he was indicted. Koroma's whereabouts are unknown, some believed he may also have been dead.

The Special Court is the first international war crimes tribunal to address the abuse of children in war. The Chief Prosecutor of the Court confirmed that far from being prosecuted for their enforced role in the war, the Court will champion children's right to live in peace by establishing crimes against children as war crimes.

5.11.   THE MEDIA

DfID supported media development and reform to promote responsible journalism. It has helped develop Sierra Leone's broadcasting policy and the general legislative framework for the media by establishing an Independent Media Commission (IMC). Through the Thompson Foundation and independent media training institutions the UK provided the necessary training for improved radio, television and print broadcasting.

More than 24 different newspaper titles are now circulated in Freetown, with a more limited circulation going to the provinces. Most journalists are freelance. Fourteen radio stations are currently operating throughout Sierra Leone including: the Sierra Leone Broadcasting Service (SLBS), its subsidiary

FM stations, and a number of independently-operated stations, including Voice of the Handicapped and believer Broadcasting Network. The British Broadcasting Corporation, Radio France International and Voice of America run a 24 hour FM broadcasts in Freetown. The IMC licenses newspapers and radio stations.

An umbrella organization of journalists called Sierra Leone Association of Journalists (SLAJ) advocates the welfare of journalists. While freelance journalists are not tied to any editorial policy, stories inevitably have a commercial value and may be bought for the headline potential rather than for investigative rigour and veracity. To enhance journalism in the country, the University of Sierra Leone, Fourah Bay College, started a very popular degree course in Journalism in 2003.

5.12. CONCLUSION

DfID, through its post-conflict reconstruction programme, has demonstrated that to sustain a war-to-peace transition beyond relief, the international community has to use resources for two overlapping purposes:

1. Programs aimed at building the structural bases for durable peace by means of projects to enhance security, justice, dispute resolution, reconciliation, gender equality, and good governance; and

2. Policies and programs to promote broadly based economic development. However, this can move forward only if government and society embrace its basic goals. Unfortunately, in the numerous instances where government and important sectors of the population have not embraced a specific peace agenda (Angola, Liberia, Israel/Palestine, Sri Lanka) the international contributions to peace are likely to be limited to local impacts.

6

ANALYSIS OF RESEARCH

ANALYSIS OF THE CAUSATIVE FACTORS AND THE IMPACT OF DFID'S POST-WAR RECONSTRUCTION PROGRAMMES IN SIERRA LEONE

6.1. INTRODUCTION

This part of the work comprises of an in-depth assessment, identifying the significant points arising from the study. This chapter places emphasis on missing gaps in research and literature in order to make tangible recommendations for further research. With reference to empirical evidence from Sierra Leone, the work refers to how factors both geographical and external influences assisted in pushing Sierra Leone towards the abyss of total collapse. The outcome of the chapter reveals limitations to the work with reference to achieving the aforementioned research goals. That is, to ascertain as to whether the DfID approach has created opportunity for change or addressed the root causes of the problems or the like. As a consequence, another area generating interest is to delve into whether the DfID approach provides the opportunity for the previously marginalized to be integrated into the decision-making process and to establish a better future.

6.2. COLD WAR EFFECT

With the slave trade being the first root and colonialism the second, it can also be inferred from literature that the consequences of the Cold War constitute a third root cause of "failed states" (Rotberg 2004). The argument is that during the Cold War smaller and weaker states like Sierra Leone were used as pawns by the Superpowers in their struggles for global hegemony. Because of the strategic and ideological considerations in this rivalry, it was easy for the importance of such states to be bloated beyond what reality would have warranted. With the end of the Cold War and the subsequent withdrawal of the so-called superpower patrons, several of the developing countries rapidly collapsed under the weight of their poverty, incapacity, lack of social cohesion and poor leadership.

In Sierra Leone, Siaka Stevens was propped up and sustained while the institutional basis of the state atrophied. The Soviet Union and the USA, and even Cuba provided him with military advisers and training at the peak of the Cold War. Tom Ofcansky, an African affairs analyst with the State Department Bureau of Intelligence and Research, revealed in an interview what had already been suspected. With the end of the Cold War and the eventual withdrawal of tens of thousands of ex-Soviet soldiers, much of Eastern Europe remained unchanged. In Africa, the collapse of the Cold War led to an eventual collapse and fragmentation of the state and the development of numerous rebel groups, which in turn led to a great demand for small arms. The availability of small arms served as a catalyst in Sierra Leone and led to a situation where conflict entrepreneurs fostered their monetary gains by targeting the disenfranchised, pretending to champion the cause of the *Lumpenproletariat*. Ofcansky noted that the youth were recruited and often drugged before battle to prepare them to wreak havoc.

6.3.   THE NATURAL RESOURCE FACTOR

The assertion that the basis of the civil war was to engage in profitable crime under the guise of warfare is supported by the fact that diamonds fuelled the conflict. Azar notes that the war was not grounded in ideology but fostered by those persuaded by the material wealth offered by Sierra Leone's diamond and mineral resources. This resulted in the view of the conflict as a result of greed rather than grievance (Azar 1990). In such case, while using warfare as a cover for criminal activity, targeting civilians was a means to an end, with the Sierra Leonean diamond mining sector being the objective.

Sierra Leone, a tiny nation, rich in natural resources, has several diamond mines, and is known for its production of gem quality diamonds (Hirsch 2001). These diamonds come from the districts of Kenema, Kono and Bo, located in the central and eastern areas of the country. Recently they have also been found in the north, specifically in Sanda Tendaren. In post-colonial Sierra Leone, diamonds have become the most important resource, accounting for 60 to 70 per cent of the government revenue (Clapham 1996) from the 1950s when they were first discovered. This gave Sierra Leone the potential for a ready source of foreign exchange. In short, as Clapham points out, "If you are looking for an African state with physical, social and economic infrastructure appropriate to success as an independent state, you would have had difficulty finding a better candidate than Sierra Leone" (ibid).

In his "greed and grievance" debate, Collier's analysis of African conflicts points to strategic minerals as the main agent responsible for the Sierra Leone's conflicts (ibid: 2000). This prompts one to wonder why countries like Botswana and Ghana, that are notably rich in diamonds and gold respectively, remain relatively peaceful. Even though he has some disagreement with Collier, Clapham agrees with the former in this respect. In defence he notes that, unlike Sierra Leone, Botswana's diamonds were derived largely from kimberlite pipes, which require sophisticated deep mining techniques and can thus be brought under control only by multinational corporations. On the other hand, Sierra Leone's diamonds are derived from alluvial deposits which make them easy to obtain for anyone with a spade and sieve who is prepared to sift through the gravel beds in which they are found. This, added to the fact that it is a resource particularly difficult to bring under state control, given its very high unit value, the relative ease with which the diamonds could be mined without needing capital or sophisticated processing and transport facilities, and the extreme ease with which they could be smuggled, made diamonds in Sierra Leone, an indicator for state failure rather than prosperity.

Historically, it is worth noting that on their discovery during colonial rule in the 1950s, diamond mines were placed under and monopolized by the Sierra Leone Selection Trust (SLST), an offshoot of De Beers, by the colonial government (Abdulah 1998). Following the collapse of the Krio, the SLST monopoly was challenged by a new group of entrepreneurs, the Lebanese, also a client of the colonial government. The Lebanese, having been boosted by the colonial government in earlier periods used their commercial linkages to the West, and with the political backing from the colonial administration and prominent Sierra Leoneans, were able to inherit the trade, which they monopolized up to the present date (Williams 2002). The third and maybe the most crucial difference between Botswana and Sierra Leone lay in the fact that Botswana had an ethnically homogenous society, which gave its politicians some assurance of their hold on power. In Sierra Leone, however, it was the opposite and with politicians desperate to cling on to power they developed a craving for illicit wealth since "access to diamond money was the critical source of leverage" (Reno 1995).

As the saying goes, 'he who controls the microphone has control over the argument'. This was true regarding the relationship between Sierra Leone's politicians, paramount chiefs and the Lebanese. The result was a patrimonial state in which politicians were willing to compromise for access to funds, further ushering Sierra Leone towards what Reno referred to as a "Shadow State" (Rotberg 2003). The eventual result, was a civil war and since 1991 the economic opportunity presented by the breakdown of law and order sustained the high levels of violence which plagued Sierra Leone (Riley 1996). However, it is worth taking into consideration that the plundering of natural resources is best achieved in an atmosphere where there is neither accountability nor means to restrain the actors (Richards 1996).

6.4.   FLAWS IN REGIME

While state collapse is recognized as providing the basic opportunity that leaders and their followers seize to pursue conflicts, the state may also subdivide into a number of specific areas where it no longer performs its core functions, making such areas vulnerable to destabilize by diverse agencies. Such was the Sierra Leone scenario. It is worth noting that not all such agencies were hostile to the state. But the fact that they performed state functions further weakened the state as much as did the rebellion itself. These functions included general order, territorial control, population control, control over armed forces, and provision of security (Jackson 1990). Sierra Leone's economic decline in the 1980s hampered the government's ability to respond effectively to the rebellion.

By the early 1990s, Sierra Leone's economy was in decline and coupled with high level corruption among state officials, the country embraced mass discontent and political instability. Political uncertainty and economic decline undermined effective policy-making and diminished public confidence in the state's ability to secure their interests and lives (Kaplan 2000). Coup plots were rife as President Momoh's sole legal party struggled to negotiate a long-delayed transition to a multiparty system. The state's security apparatus was also ineffective as wages failed to keep up with inflation or remained unpaid for weeks. Army morale sunk to low levels, as soldiers began moonlighting and joined in the looting and harassment of the peasantry. The net effect was a government that had to turn to foreign actors for security assistance (Francis 2005).

Involvement in the Liberian Civil War increased from 1991 until Sierra Leone became simply a theatre in that conflict, with little control over its own territory. Military units from Nigeria and Guinea joined the Sierra Leone army in mid 1991 and helped to recapture back several towns from the RUF (Abdullah 1998). This infuriated Taylor who threatened attacks on Lungi airport and launched cross border raids in support of the rebels. Sierra Leonean troops responded with their own attacks on rebel bases inside Liberia. Sierra Leone by default had become a new front of the Liberian conflict and so by May 1992, the Nigerian and Guinean presence was transformed into a regular ECOMOG mission. On the other side were ULIMO and remnants of Doe-loyalists who had fled to Sierra Leone and joined in counter-offensive measures against Taylor's forces (Reno 1995). The Sierra Leonean government's failure to exercise control over such elements provided an excuse for Taylor's retaliations that fuelled the escalation and occasionally tipped the scales in the RUF's favour.

6.5   PRIVATISATION OF SECURITY FUNCTIONS

The privatisation and alienation of security functions have been specific results of Sierra Leone's failure. With the collapse of the army, the government increasingly relied on private and foreign security agencies for protection, many of which were also affiliated with mining firms. These actors "privatised" the conflict and introduced the ethos of commercial profit seeking as a major current underlying the conflict (Musah/Fayemi 2000). The government's need to elicit the help of private security was exacerbated by two additional factors—first, the inadequacy of assistance received from ECOMOG and UNAMSI; Second, the imposition of a UN arms embargo on all parties to the conflict. The effectiveness of ECOMOG and UNAMSIL was hampered by the absence of a UN Security Council authorization to use force (Nwokedi 1992). The foreign forces also lacked adequate knowledge of the terrain as well as the capacity to deal with the guerrilla tactics employed so efficiently by the RUF. Fluctuations in numbers caused by periodic troop withdrawals by some contributors also meant that the peacekeepers were not a reliable security force for the Sierra Leonean government. Private security firms therefore had to be employed to supplement the peacekeepers and provide strategic training for the Sierra Leone army.

As a consequence of this, Executive Outcomes (EO), a South African Private Military Corporation (PMC) recruited by the National Provisional Ruling Council in a complex deal to supplement the army, was marked for criticism (Reno 1995). In the deal, the nearly bankrupt government, in need of access to the country's wealth, allowed a diamond mining company to pay EO for the cost of their military operation, in return for access to diamond areas captured by EO. The outcome was very successful, with EO being able to establish their military superiority in just a year after their arrival in 1995. In March 1996, EO's presence was strong enough to hold a successful election (Collier et al. 2003).

In assuming power, President Kabbah became very dependent on EO for security and in dealing with the conflict at the expense of the army. It also led to Kabbah taking more seriously the demands of outside mediators who argued that the Sierra Leone's marauding army was undermining his government's legitimacy (Reno 1995). The result was a government attempt to distance itself from the army and develop an alliance with the Kamajors, a militia group of Mende background. Furthermore, in a desperate attempt to reverse the situation, Kabbah went further to polarise the stance of the army by approving a radical cut in army enlistment and diversion of resources from them. This led to the army attempting three coups and finally joining the RUF after being disbanded by the Kabbah government (Bundu 2001).

It was at this juncture of the conflict that the government decided to take a u-turn from pursuing a military victory with the help of EO to that of a peaceful path through the Abidjan Peace Accord in November 1996. There it was agreed that EO should be withdrawn despite its effectiveness in fighting the RUF. On the contrary, the RUF resumed its resistance following the withdrawal of EO from Sierra Leone in 1997, rendering the agreement completely worthless. The lack of an effective army or the delegitimisation of the army turns on its head the Weberian notion of state, where the state has a monopoly on the legitimate use of force. A monopoly becomes a liability when the government is unable also to monopolise the extracting of resources still available from the diamond-mining sector to finance its war operations (Reno 1995). As a result, the government was left with no option but to privatise the army again to another category of private specialty entities willing to provide security for mining operations and to pay the government in cash or in kind for a role in the diamond fields. Groups such as Diamond Works and its subsidiary, Branch Energy, had to find their own security for mining operations in the Koindu area. Other commercial mining operations secured assistance from a wide array of private specialty groups (examples include British companies such as Lifeguard, the Gurkhas, Defence Systems Ltd, Sky Air, Occidental, and American companies such as Military Professional Resources Inc [MPRI] and International Charters Inc.). Most of these commercial and security firms also had important connections with major players in the conflict and this further complicated the roles of those players in the search for a solution. The subsequent failure of the government to monopolise both factors and the privatisation of the security function to mercenary groups can be seen as a factor in the failure.

6.6.   POLITICAL INSTABILITY

The proliferation of political parties particularly on the side of the government, characterized the Sierra Leone conflict. Political instability fed uncertainty and often benefited the rebels who took the opportunity to form alliances with supporters of ousted or removed regimes. Sierra Leone had five different governments in the decade since the outbreak of violence (Bundu 2001). Each of the post-Momoh regimes came to power promising a swift end to the war and proceeded to reach out to the rebels with upgrades in offers that yielded no corresponding dividends. The RUF also suffered its share of political uncertainties, so it became difficult to know with whom to negotiate and on whom to rely for implementation of an agreement. A rift between Sankoh loyalists and followers of Sam Bockarie unsettled peace agreements in 1996, although it did little to weaken the RUF (Hirsch 2001). Attempts in March 1997 to remove Sankoh (who had been detained in Nigeria) from the RUF leadership weakened negotiations. Such political uncertainties disrupt peace efforts, delay the implementation of agreements, and provide opportunities for escalation. Use of unconventional tactics in the conflict frustrated the government army and its supporters, many of whom lacked training and experience in guerrilla warfare.

The collapse of the Sierra Leonean state began soon after independence in 1961. Sierra Leoneans refer to the regime of President Siaka Stevens, who established a socialist one-party state from 1968 to 1985, as the "17-year plague of locusts" (Hirsch 2001). Successive regimes merely accelerated the country's slide into economic atrophy and anarchy. Swarms of "locusts" stripped government agencies of anything of value. Reduced to an empty shell, the government even lacked the funds to print money (Reno 1995). Civil servants, teachers, and police went without pay and invented various fraudulent devices to survive. Scores of ghost workers were added to the government payroll and their salaries were collected by living workers. In one government department 75 per cent of the staff were found to be nonexistent. State institutions collapsed and the country's only radio broadcasting tower was carted off and sold by a bureaucrat, depriving the President of the ability to speak to the people (ibid). When it started in 1991, Sankoh's Revolutionary United Front (RUF) was originally a rebellion against the vampire state. But they quickly earned the opprobrium of the people as they rampaged across the country, killing, raping, and hacking off the limbs of innocent people. Women and children who stood in their way were not spared (Richards, 1996).

6.7.   THE PEACEKEEPING ELEMENT

The UN did not authorize the intervention to use force in its operation, even though it is established under its Chapter VII (United Nations Resolution 1999a). It is alleged that it cooperated too closely with ECOMOG troops who were considered as being biased towards the government (Alao 1999). These were issues that limited the effectiveness of UNAMSIL. It is likely that a proper identification of the rebels as the villains in the conflict could have helped to authorize an intervention whose sole purpose was to help the legitimate and democratically elected government of Sierra Leone regain control of its territory and population, restore its state, and end the rebel insurgency. After the UNOMSIL debacle at the end of 1998 and the authorization of UNAMSIL in 1999, the UN should also have authorized a change in mandate to peace enforcement (Olonisakin 2000). Such a move could have averted the embarrassing episodes of hostage-taking that continue to plague the mission. The UN intervention in Sierra Leone was instrumental in legitimizing the Lome Agreement that endorsed the RUF as a partner in government (Adebajo 2002). That agreement was largely unpopular among civil society as it banned on-going efforts to put the RUF leadership on trial for human rights violations. The presence of UNAMSIL, however, facilitated the repatriation of some refugees and helped the government's effort to raise funds for reconstruction. Despite its ineffectiveness as a military force, the intervention helped bring much needed credibility to the peace process. Unfortunately that process was not used to end the crisis in Sierra Leone.

The first UN intervention had a clear exit plan. It was mandated for a period of six months subject to review as necessary. When the conflict intensified to a point where the mandate for the intervention appeared to be untenable, UNAMSIL quickly withdrew. The second instalment, on the other hand, entered with an open-ended commitment to monitor the implementation of the Lome Agreement (ibid). The UN Security Council did not modify its rules of engagement even as its forces came under persistent RUF attack. Contributing states such as India therefore withdrew their troops when they

110

perceived the intervention as unhelpful to their interests. Such unilateral withdrawals hurt the overall purposes of the mission, although it was the only way contributing states could exit the process in the absence of a general UN policy on collective exit (United Nations Resolution 1999a). The mission's principal goal of facilitating the implementation of the Lome Agreement was largely unattained. This was due to its ineffectiveness and the government's continued weakness in the face of RUF atrocities (Abdullah 1998).

The British intervention, dubbed 'Operation Palliser', was triggered by the "disappearance" of 500 United Nations peacekeepers in Sierra Leone (http://en.wikipedia.org/wiki/ Sierra_Leone.12/10/04). The withdrawal of ECOMOG troops in late April 2000 created a huge security vacuum that United Nations peacekeepers under Force Commander Vijay Jetley of India were unable to fill. The RUF exploited the situation to escalate its attacks on the UNAMSIL. Five hundred UN troops were taken prisoners by the RUF in May, prompting the UK to dispatch a "rescue" force to the country. The British deployment came in the aftermath of the major clashes of the war and as Taylor's Liberia, a major backer of the RUF, was seeking international legitimacy and therefore had become a less visible threat. The presence of the United Nations force (UNAMSIL) also eased the British entry by helping to legitimatize the intervention. The intervention comprised 800 paratroopers, with strong air force and naval support.

The British intervention sought to realize several immediate and long-term goals. In the short term, the mission sought to reverse RUF gains and change the conflict structure in favour of pro-government forces. To accomplish this, it launched an operation to rescue the 500 missing United Nations peacekeepers and also to repel the imminent RUF capture of Waterloo and possibly Freetown (BBC, 11/10/04). To save Freetown, troops were dispatched to secure the local airport and then deployed throughout the capital and its environs as a buffer to the RUF offensive. The long-term goals were geared toward capacity building assistance to help pro-government forces consolidate the gains of peace and security. To this end, the British troops provided technical training and assistance to the Sierra Leone army that had been in complete disarray following the sudden death of its Nigerian Chief of Staff, General Maxwell Khobe in April 2000. British experts also assisted the UN in tactical planning and strategic deployments as well as with logistics such as helicopters to transport Jordanian peacekeepers to defensive positions.

The British mission was short-lived and geared toward the accomplishment of relatively limited goals. It gave a much-needed boost to government forces but nevertheless produced little lasting effect. Its capacity development program was crucial to the emergence of UNAMSIL as a credible force in Sierra Leone. However, longstanding operational difficulties as well as the UN's reluctance to authorize the use of force robbed the UN mission of opportunities to reverse RUF gains in the conflict (Zartman 1995a). The military and non-military balance remained constant over the period of intervention, even though the intervention evolved into a technical support group later and its size was drastically reduced to 251 members. It is certain that the British originally intended for the intervention to be a "rescue mission". It was supposed to be a short, precise, trouble-shooting mission that would avoid mission creep, deliver quickly, and exit as soon as possible. However, events on the ground convinced the British to tackle capacity building as a way of ensuring that their exit would not create an imbalance similar to the one created by the ECOWAS disengagement.

The immediate goals were better defined and hence easier to achieve than the long-term ones. As a direct result of the intervention, the RUF was forced to release the 500 UN hostages. The British impact was felt again, in late August 2000 when the West Side Boys (a pro-AFRC faction originally supportive of the government) abducted eleven British soldiers and a Sierra Leonean as leverage for the release of their leader (BBC, 6 January 2003). The British troops intervened to secure their release just as the United Nations was dealt a heavy blow by India's announcement of a pullout. British assistance was also directly responsible for the successful deployment of the Jordanian UN contingent in Sierra Leone. Without their helicopters and operational cover, the Jordanian troops could have become stranded or restricted to non-contested terrain while the RUF continued to devastate the diamond-rich northwest. In terms of long-term goals, the impact of the British intervention was quite muted, above all because of the advanced stage of disrepair into which the government army had fallen before the intervention. Poor training and lack of adequate equipment was exacerbated by petty quarrels among the ranks and with allies such as the Kamajor militias. British capacity-building effort yielded better results for UNAMSIL, which became more professional and handled superbly the rescue of 233 peacekeepers (mainly from India) held hostage by RUF in Kailahun soon after the British intervention.

It can be concluded that military intervention is not the best approach to conflict resolution as it takes a state from failure to collapse (Bundu 2001).

ECOMOG participated in looting Liberia (Aning 1999) and also diamonds in Sierra Leone. The conflict began due to the failure of governance, the dissolution of the economy, and the breakdown of the social fabric in Sierra Leone, and will only end when these elements are restored (Zartman 2004). The Sierra Leone experience raises serious questions about the non-military side of the conflict management operation. Conflict management "doctrine" indicates that one can only end a conflict by negotiating with one's enemy and that any party to the problem must be a party to the solution; yet there are limits, if not on the participants, at least on the conditions under which their participation can be envisaged. Some enemies are beyond the pale, incapable of making and holding an acceptable agreement (Stedman 2002). The deliberate atrocities of the RUF, whose hallmark was amputation, characterised them as objects of punishment, and not freedom fighters or one interested in power-sharing. What about Renamo of Mozambique (Chase-Dunn/Manning 2002); UNITA in Angola; Taylor's NPFL (Aning 1999); the Palestinians or the Israelis in the Middle East? It is too easy to qualify one's enemy as beyond the pale and not worthy of negotiation.

6.8.   MULTI-PARTY DEMOCRACY OR ETHNICITY?

Following the resumption of the conflict, the British government pushed for early elections which Kabbah won in the face of lack of a genuine democracy movement. Kabbah's nearest rival, Ernest Koroma of the All People's Congress (APC) won 27 seats. The last two seats were taken by former junta leader Johnny Paul Koroma's Peace and Liberation Party (PLP), which presented problem on two fronts: first, Koroma was widely expected to be indicted for war crimes and crimes against humanity for incidents that occurred during the war and secondly, 70% of his votes came from a special ballot cast by the army. The candidate of the RUFP - the RUF's political evolution - Pallo Bangura - received less than 2% of votes and his party failed to gain a single seat. However, Bangura declared that RUFP would accept the people's verdict. President Ahmed Tejan Kabbah was re-elected and the governing SLPP retained its parliamentary majority in May 2002.

The result however was a deep domestic dissatisfaction, particularly among the younger generation with respect to corruption, tribalism, age factor and the indifferent nature of its government. Rather than preventing decay, elections accelerated it by openly encouraging competition which in the absence of a genuine democratic platform leads to conflict. It is worth noting that a lack of democratic political culture over a long period of time until 1996 and the practice of a politics of exclusion of youth and certain ethnic groups, nepotism, and tribalism that are at play in pre war Sierra Leone, led to antagonism that caused the war in the first place. There is also lack of structure and clear-cut political ideology by parties in Sierra Leone. Many people believe that a de facto one party rule is presently in operation due to the overwhelming majority of the SLPP in Parliament. This has rendered parliament ineffective and MPs are not able to represent effectively their constituencies.

This was also the case in the 1996 election which was expected to produce stable governments in Sierra Leone. In the period leading to the first election in 1996 and the previous election in 2002, DfID forced 'democracy' on a large section of the society that had requested "Peace Before Election" in the PEBEC campaign led by Hylton Fyle. Fyle's campaign was for power sharing and not winner takes all elections, a disturbing characterisation of democratic, competitive election. With hindsight, it may not be wrong to say that the British government and its DfID made a big mistake in pushing for elections and thus failed to see the larger picture, that is, the transition from authoritarianism to stable democracy is a very disruptive process in itself since it encourages the conflict that exists underground to manifest itself freely, but without the checks and balances, and the restraint of a well established democratic system. The complex situation following triggered by the elections created highly undesirable side effects such as the killing and amputation of more people in post-elections, thereby placing emphasis on the conundrum of democratization in a collapsed state (ICG 2003: 1, 2004: 24). Therefore one may argue that state collapse was not the best place for Sierra Leonean democracy to have started.

6.9.   REINSTATEMENT OF COLONIAL STATE SYSTEM

Another very controversial issue is the reinstatement of the chiefs. In the previous chapter I have argued that despite pressure for decentralization and a move away from the practice of the past, Kabbah convinced the British government to support the rebuilding of the paramount chief system, which traditionally was the lowest level of administration and which covered the entire country except the area around the capital, Freetown. It had been the basis of rule of British colonial authorities.

Traditionally, chiefs handled dispute resolution and tax collection. Because of the war, 63 of the 149 paramount chiefs had been killed or died, and nearly all the others had fled from their areas. DfID in 2000 established a paramount chief's restoration programme, which, among other things, built houses for 50 chiefs (DfID 2002). Elections to fill the 63 vacancies were held in late 2002 and early 2003; taxpayers (mostly men) elect councillors who then elect the paramount chiefs, who hold the position for life (Malan et al. 2003). Within Sierra Leone, however, there were substantial objections to the programme. Chiefs are seen as being an important cause of the war, through their corruption and alienation of the youth. As long ago as 1955-56 (during colonial times) there were uprisings against the abuses of power of chiefs and their demand for illegal taxes and fees, which were described by a commission then as 'a civil war rather than a disturbance' (quoted in Fanthorpe 2001). The World Bank (2003: 44) reports that 'chiefs' rule has led to mismanagement, power abuse and failure to ensure the delivery of decentralized services'. DfID (2002: 35) notes that 'over the last 20 or 30 years, this [customary court] system has fallen into decay and been the subject of considerable abuses'. Reinstating them by and large is to many, a reinstatement of colonial rule and thus raises the question of neo-colonialism. Glentworth (2002) notes: "local people and particularly women and the youth are no longer prepared to put up with the kind of exploitation that they previously suffered" under the chiefs.

Findings from my field work have pointed to the need to redress the bias of customary law and social system at the village and chiefdom levels which protect the 'influential' at the expense of the poor and vulnerable. In particular, the Forced Labour Ordinance of 1932 remains in force, allowing chiefs and their extended families to force young people and outsiders to work for them (Moore et al. 2003: 22). DfID (2002: 87) admits that the chiefdom system can succeed only if there are 'new relationships between the chiefs and their people. Chieftaincy can only really be effective and accepted if chiefs' behaviour avoids repeat of past mistakes—vindictive and exploitative punishments through the courts, arbitrary seizure of land and property, etc. Chiefs in diamond mining areas are using the 0.75 per cent diamond tax they receive for personal gain instead of, as intended, for the benefit of the community (Malan et al. 2003).

Chiefs are using aid money for personal enrichment and to reward political supporters (Fanthorpe 2001). Chiefs are also complaining that the British-built houses are not grand enough and not compatible with their status: Paramount Chief Sigismond Caulker Quebboka told the *Salone Times* (5 Feb. 2004) that he cannot stay in a house with such small rooms and no parlour. The return of chiefs has brought tensions in some areas as the government also tries to restore civil administration. Some chiefs are refusing to cooperate with district officers and there are conflicts with local governments elected in 2004 (Malan 2004a). Zack-Williams (1999) argues that Britain has chosen to rectify and rebuild a discredited feudal tradition and delay the development of grassroots democracy. Archibald and Richards (2002: 358, 360) note that "standard NGO practice in post-war Sierra Leone" is to work with village development committees (VDCs). The problem is "that VDCs were invariably comprised of elders and members of elites who excluded some groups and individuals. 'In a majority of cases VDC members had registered themselves as the 'most needy' residents or (allegedly) diverted inputs to their kin residing in urban areas. IDPs women and youths were excluded because they had no representatives (or 'friends') on the committee".

6.10.   CONCLUSION

This study is set out to address the mind-boggling questions concerning the inability of International community, the state of Sierra Leone and its institutions to resolve the civil war. The study has already showed that, Donor-led post-war reconstruction programmes tend to reinforce earlier social structure and a return to the status quo rather than create opportunities for the previously marginalised.

This brief overview of some of the factors responsible for Sierra Leone's conflict has demonstrated that in order for action to be taken for reconstructing failed states, it is imperative that the global and local alliances making for state collapse be taken into consideration. The study has raised interesting discourses while also painting a vivid picture of the multifaceted factors that are responsible for the conflict. Any action therefore to address them must seek to correlate with the challenges they face.

Also, it can be concluded that third party intervention in such conflicts as that of the Sierra Leone case, do not necessarily resolve the conflict. Instead, it exacerbates the conflict situation because of the mutual suspicion of the third party. Governments battling internal strife such as Sierra Leone are quick to either accuse the mediator(s) as interfering in domestic affairs or accused of supporting rebel insurgency. Rebels usually see the third party intervention as necessarily geared toward supporting the embattling government.

The conflict in Sierra Leone, as the study already revealed, failed because of the emphasis put on post-war reconstruction to the detriment of addressing the fundamental root causes of the conflict. In that situation, the conflict is not truly resolved. Donor-led post-war reconstruction or interventions are interested in the absence violence. But, absence of violence does not mean peace, but negative peace. For, the injustices that culminated in the conflict remained unresolved

The study also showed that, conflicts such as that of Sierra Leone could not have been resolved by only military intervention. But it needed all parties either directly or indirectly involved in the conflict to agree on the need for peace as a sufficient condition for resolving the conflict. Other important considerations for peace include the need to address issues of bad governance, corruption justice for the marginalised and their like. If all these factors are put on the table for negotiation, may not only lead to an effective post-war reconstruction, but a strong foundation for nation building.

6.11.   RECOMMENDATIONS

On the basis of the findings of this study, the following suggestions are offered. The rationale is to serve as a guideline for policy debate and for institutions committed to peace-building in Sierra Leone and else where in the African Continent.

Firstly, it is recommended that, persons who consciously or unconsciously contributed to the civil war, maimed and killed law-abiding citizens, must be arrested and prosecuted by either the International Criminal Court or the local courts in Sierra Leone. This would be the first step in the resolution of the Sierra Leonean conflict; rather than enduring the ongoing management and escalating cost by the state.

Secondly, it is recommended that, Donor-led post-war reconstruction should be interested in unearthing the root cause(s) of the pre-war. This will enable such issues to be addressed when negotiating with the warring factions. Funds should be channelled through accredited foreign or domestic NGOs to champion the post-war reconstruction efforts. This will be a better option than put funds in the hands of a government that is unable to assert its authority to its own territory. The danger is that, such funding may be used to buy more weapons to fight the insurgents.

Thirdly, it is suggested that, intervening in conflicts such as that of Sierra Leone, need a better understanding of the local people and the dynamics of the conflict before any meaningful intervention could be made. To this end, all persons or warring factions should be identified and brought to the negotiation table. Sidelining anyone of the factions in the conflict has the potential to ravel to peace process.

Finally, adequate compensation should be paid to citizens who suffered before and during the conflict by the state. Those who lost their relations if possible, should be compensated by the state. Those, whose livelihood has been cut short as a result of deformity, should be cared for by the state.

BIBLIOGRAPHY

Abdullah, Ibrahim (1998). <u>Bush Path to Destruction: The Origin and Character of the Revolutionary United Front/Sierra Leone</u>. In: The Journal of Modern African Studies 36:2 (1998), pp. 203-235.

Abdullah, Ibrahim (ed.) (2004). <u>Between Democracy and Terror: The Sierra Leone Civil War</u>. Dakar: Council for the Development of Social Science Research in Africa.

Abdullah, Ibrahim and Patrick Muana (1998). <u>The Revolutionary United Front of Sierra Leone: A Revolt of the Lumpenproletariat</u>. In: Christopher Clapham (ed.). African Guerrillas. Oxford: James Currey, pp. 172-193.

Abraham, Arthur (1978). <u>Mende Government and Politics under Colonial Rule: A Historical Study of Political Change in Sierra Leone, 1890-1937</u>. Freetown: Sierra Leone University Press.

Adebajo, Adekeye (1999). <u>Pax Nigeriana? ECOMOG in Liberia, 1990-1997</u>. Oxford: Faculty of Social Studies, University of Oxford.

Adebajo, Adekeye (2002). <u>Liberia's Civil War: Nigeria, ECOMOG, and Regional Security in West Africa</u>. Boulder; London: Lynne Rienner Publishers.

Adebajo, Adekeye (2004). <u>West Africa's Tragic Twins: Building Peace in Liberia and Sierra Leone</u>. In: Keating, Thomas F. and W. Andy Knight (eds.). Building Sustainable Peace, Edmonton: The University of Alberta Press, pp. 167-188.

Adler, Peter (1987). <u>Membership Roles in Field Research.</u> Qualitative Research Methods Series 6. London: Sage Publications.

Ake, Claude (1967). <u>A Theory of Political Integration.</u> Dorsey Press.

Alao, Abiodun (1999). <u>The Problem of the Failed State in Africa.</u> In: Muthiah, Alagappa and Takashi Inoguchi (eds.). International Security

Management and the United Nations. Tokyo: United Nations University Press, pp. 83-102.

Alao, Abiodun, John Mackinlay and Funmi Olonisakin (1999). Peacekeepers, Politicians and Warlords: The Liberian Peace Process. New York; Paris; Tokyo: United Nations University Press. Alden, Wily L. and S. Mbaya (2001). Land People and Forests in Eastern and Southern Africa at the Beginning of the 21st Century: The Impact of Land Relations on the Role of Communities in Forest Future. Nairobi: IUCN-EARO.

Alger, Chadwick F. and Judit Balazs (1985). Conflict and Crisis of International Order: New Tasks of Peace Research: Proceedings of the International Peace Research Association, Tenth General Conference. Budapest: Centre for Peace Research Coordination of the Hungarian Academy of Sciences.

Alie, Joe A. D. (1990). A New History of Sierra Leone. New York: St. Martin's Press.
Amin, Samir and Francis McDonagh (1973). Neo-Colonialism in West Africa. Harmondsworth: Penguin Books.

Anderson, Mary B. (1999). Do No Harm: How Aid Can Support Peace - or War. Boulder; London: Lynne Rienner Publishers.

Aning, Emmanuel Kwesi (1994). Managing Regional Security in West Africa: ECOWAS, ECOMOG, and Liberia. Copenhagen: Centre for Development Research.

Aning, Emmanuel Kwesi (1999a). Security in the West African Subregion: An Analysis of ECOWAS' Policies in Liberia. Copenhagen: Institute of Political Science, University of Copenhagen.

Aning, Emmanuel Kwesi (1999b). Eliciting Compliance from Warlords: The ECOWAS Experience in Liberia, 1990-1997. In: Review of African Political Economy 26:81 (1999).

Archibald, S. and Paul Richards (2002). Conversion to Human Rights? Popular Debate About War and Justice in Rural Central Sierra Leone. In: Africa 2002.

Ayoob, Mohammed (1995). The Third World Security Predicament: State Making, Regional Conflict and the International System. Boulder: Lynne Rienner Publishers.

Ayoob, Mohammed (1996). State-making, State Breaking and State Failure: Explaining the Roots of Third World Insecurity. In: Van de Goor, Luc et al. (eds.). Between Development and Destruction: An Inquiry Into the Causes of Conflict in Post-Colonial Societies. New York: St. Martin's Press.

Ayoob, Mohammed (1999). From Regional System to Regional Society: Exploring Key Variables in the Construction of Regional Order. In: Australian Journal of International Affairs 53:3 (1999), pp. 247–260.

Ayoob, Mohammed and Kandury Subrahmanyam (1972). The Liberation War. New Delhi: S. Chand & Co.

Azar, Edward E. (1972). Conflict Escalation and Conflict Reduction in International Crisis: Suez, 1956. In: Journal of Conflict Resolution 16:2 (1972), pp. 183-201.

Azar, Edward E. (1980). The Conflict and Peace Data Bank (COPDAB) Project. In: Journal of Conflict Resolution 24:1 (1980), pp. 143-152.

Azar, Edward E. (1990). The Management of Protracted Social Conflict: Theory and Cases. Aldershot: Dartmouth Pub. Co.

Azar, Edward E. (1991). The Analysis and Management of Protracted Social Conflict. In: Volkan, J. D., J. V. Montville and D. A. Julius (eds.). The Psychodynamics of International Relationships. Vol. II: Unofficial Diplomacy at Work. Lexington, MA: Lexington Books, pp. 93-120.
Azar, Edward E. and John W. Burton (1986). International Conflict Resolution: Theory and Practice. Sussex: Wheatsheaf.

Azar, Edward E. and Thomas Sloan (1975). Dimensions of Interaction: A Source Book for the Study of the Behavior of 31 Nations From 1948 Through 1973. Pittsburgh, PA: The International Studies Association.

Bain, William (2001). Trusteeship: A Response to Failed States. Paper presented at the Conference on Failed States and Global Governance, Organised by Purdue University, April 10-14, 2001, Florence, Italy.

Baker, Mona (2006). Translation and Conflict: A Narrative Account. Milton Park Abingdon; New York: Routledge.

Baker, Pauline H. and John Ausink (1996). State Collapse and Ethnic Violence: Toward a Predictive Model. In: Parameters 26:1 (1996), pp. 19-36.

Bannon, Ian and Paul Collier (eds.) (2003). Natural Resources and Violent Conflict: Options and Actions. Washington, D.C.: The World Bank.

Bebler, Anton A. (1973). Military rule in Africa: Dahomey, Ghana, Sierra Leone, and Mali. New York: Praeger Publishers Inc.

Beck, Cheryl T. (2005). Benefits of Participating in Internet Interviews: Women Helping Women. In: Qualitative Health Research 15:3 (2005), pp. 411-422.

Becker, Howard S. (1970). Sociological Work: Method and Substance, Chicago: Aldine Pub. Co.

Bellamy, Alex J., Paul Williams and Stuart Griffin (2004). Understanding Peacekeeping. Cambridge: Polity.

Berg, Bruce L. (1988). Qualitative Research Methods for the Social Sciences. Hemel Hempstead: Allyn & Bacon.

Berg, Bruce L. (2009). Qualitative Research Methods for the Social Sciences. 7th ed. Upper Saddle River, N.J.: Pearson Prentice Hall.

Bertram, Eva (1995). Reinventing Governments: The Promise and Perils of United Nations Peace Building. In: Journal of Conflict Resolution 39:5, pp. 387-418.

Best, Samuel J., and Brian Krueger (2002). New Approaches to Assessing Opinion: The Prospects for Electronic Mail Surveys. In: International Journal of Public Opinion Research 14:1, pp. 73-92.

Brazaitis, Mark, John Coyne and Karl Luntta (1999). Living on the Edge: Fiction by Peace Corps Writers. Willimantic, Conn.: Curbstone Press.
Bredel, Ralf (2003). Long-Term Conflict Prevention and Industrial Development: The United Nations and Its Specialized Agency, UNIDO. United Nations Industrial Development Organization. Leiden: Brill; Boston: Martinus Nijhoff.

Brown, Michael E. (1996). The International Dimensions of Internal Conflict. Cambridge, Mass.: MIT Press.

Brownlie, Ian (1998). The Rule of Law in International Affairs: International Law at the Fiftieth Anniversary of the United Nations. The Hague; London; Boston: Martinus Nijhoff Publishers.

Bryman, Alan (2001). Social Research Methods. New York: Oxford University Press Inc.

Bryman, Alan and Duncan Cramer (1994). Quantitative Data Analysis for Social Scientists. London: Routledge.

Budd, Eric N. (2004). Democratization, Development, and the Patrimonial State in the Age of Globalization. Lanham, MD: Lexington Books.

Bulmer, Martin (1984). Sociological Research Methods. 2nd edn. New Brunswick: Transaction Books.

Bundu, Abass (2001). Democracy by Force?: A Study of International Military Intervention in the Civil War in Sierra Leone from 1991-2000. London: Universal Publishers.

Burawoy, Michael (ed.) (2000). Global Ethnography: Forces, Connections and Imaginations in a Postmodern World. Berkeley, LA; London: University of California Press.

Burton, John (1979). Deviance, Terrorism, and War: The Process of Solving Unsolved Social and Political Problems. New York: St Martins Press.

Burton, John (1990a). Conflict: Resolution and Prevention. New York: St. Martins   Press.

Burton, John (1990b). Conflict: Basic Human Needs. New York: St. Martins Press.

Buzan, Barry (1991). People, States, and Fear: An Agenda for International Security Studies in the Post-Cold War Era. London: Harvester Wheatsheaf.

Cabrita, João M. (2000). Mozambique: The Tortuous Road to Democracy. Basingstoke: Palgrave.

Carment, C. (2003). Assessing State Failure: Implications for Theory and Policy. In: Third World Quaterly 24:3 (2003), pp. 407-427.

Carment, David and Frank Harvey (2000). Using Force to Prevent Ethnic Violence. Westport, CN: Praeger Press.

Carment, David and Frank Harvey (2001). Using Force to Prevent Ethnic Violence: An Evaluation of Theory and Evidence. Westport, London: Praeger Publishers Inc.

Carment, David and Patrick James (eds.) (1997). Wars in the Midst of Peace: The International Politics of Ethnic Conflict. Pittsburgh: University of Pittsburgh Press.

Carment, David, Patrick James and Zeynap Taydas (eds.) (2006). Who Intervenes?: Ethnic Conflict and Interstate Crisis. Columbus: Ohio State University Press.

Chandler, David (1999). Bosnia: Faking Democracy after Dayton. Pluto Press.

Chapman, William (2002). Vientiane, Laos: Lane Xang's Capital in the Age of Modernization and Globalization. In: Logan, William S. (2002). The Disappearing 'Asian' City: Protecting Asia's Urban Heritage in a Globalizing World. Oxford; New York: Oxford University Press.

Chase-Dunn, C. and E. Susan Manning (2002). City Systems and World-Systems: Four Millennia of City Growth and Decline. In: Cross-Cultural Research 36:4 (2002), pp.379-398.

Chege, Michael (2002). Sierra Leone: The State that Came Back from the Dead.
In: The Washington Quarterly 25:3 (2002), pp. 147-160.

Clapham, Christopher (1976). Liberia and Sierra Leone: An Essay in Comparative Politics. Cambridge: Cambridge University Press.

Clapham, Christopher (1996). Africa and the International System: The Politics of State Survival. Cambridge: Cambridge University Press.

Clapham, Christopher (1998). Degrees of Statehood. In: Review of International Studies 24 (1998), pp. 143–57.

Clapham, Christopher (2004). The Decay and Attempted Reconstruction of African Territorial Statehood. University of Leipzig Papers on Africa: Politics and Economics 69. Leipzig: Inst. fuer Afrikanistik.

Collier, Paul (2003). Civil War as Development in Reverse. In: Collier, Paul, V. L. Elliott, Havard Hegre, Anke Hoeffler, Marta Reynal-Querol, and Nicholas Sambanis. Breaking the Conflict Trap: Civil War and Development

Policy. World Bank Policy Research Reports. Oxford: World Bank/Oxford University Press.

Collier, Paul, V. L. Elliott, Havard Hegre, Anke Hoeffler, Marta Reynal-Querol, and Nicholas Sambanis (2003). Breaking the Conflict Trap: Civil War and Development Policy. World Bank Policy Research Reports. Oxford: World Bank/Oxford University Press.

Collier, Paul and Anke Hoeffler (2000). Greed and Grievance in Civil War. Oxford: Institute of Economics and Statistics, Centre for the Study of African Economies, University of Oxford.

Collier, Paul and Anke Hoeffler (2002). Greed and Grievance in Civil War. Oxford: Institute of Economics and Statistics, Centre for the Study of African Economies, University of Oxford.

Conteh-Morgan, Earl and Mac Dixon-Fyle (1999). Sierra Leone at the End of the Twentieth Century: History, Politics and Society. New York: Peter Lang.

Chong, Daniel P. L. (2003). UNTAC in Cambodia: A New Model for Humanitarian Aid in Failed States? In: Milliken, Jennifer (ed.). State Failure, Collapse and Reconstruction. Oxford: Blackwell, pp.201 – 222.

Conteh Morgan, Earl and Karl P. Magyar (eds.) (1998). Peacekeeping in Africa: ECOMOG in Liberia. Basingstoke: Macmillan.

Corbin, Juliet M. and Anselm L. Strauss (eds.) (1993). Grounded Theory in Practice. Thousand Oaks, CA: Sage Publications.

Corbin, Juliet M. and Anselm L. Strauss (1998). Basics of Qualitative Research: Techniques and Procedures for Developing Grounded Theory. 2nd ed. Thousand Oaks, CA: Sage Publications.

Coser, Lewis A. (1956). The Functions of Social Conflict. London: Routledge & Kegan Paul.

Cusick, Linda, Anthea Martin and Tiggey May (2003). Vulnerability and Involvement in Drug Use and Sex Work. Home Office Research Study 268. London: Home Office Research, Development and Statistics Directorate.

Dearth, Douglas H. (1996). Failed States: An International Conundrum. In: Defence Intelligence Journal 5:2, pp. 119-130.

Deng, Francis M. (1996). Sovereignty as Responsibility: Conflict Management in Africa. Washington, D.C.: The Brookings Institution.

Deng, Francis M. and I. William Zartman (2002). A Strategic Vision for Africa: The Kampala Movement. Washington, D.C.: The Brookings Institution.

De Fragoso Vidal, Nuno C. (2002). Post-modern Patrimonialism in Africa. London: University of London.

DfID (2002a). Sierra Leone Governance Reconstruction and Reform Progress Report. Internal report. London: DfID West Africa Department.

DfID (2002b). Sierra Leone: Governance Reconstruction and Reform Progress Report. Internal Report. London: DfID West Africa Department.

DfID (2004). Evaluation of the Conflict Prevention Pools: Sierra Leone. DFID Evaluation Report EV 647. <http://www.dfid.gov.uk/aboutdfid/performance/files/ ev647sleone.pdf> Rev. 2009-03-15.

Dobbins, James et al. (2003). America's Role in Nation-Building: From Germany to Iraq. Santa Monica, CA: RAND Corporation. <http://www.rand.org/ publications/MR/MR1753/> Rev. 2009-03-19.

Dobbins, James (2005). The UN's Role in Nation-Building: From the Congo to Iraq. Santa Monica, CA: RAND Corporation.

Dool, Abdullahi (1998). Failed States: When Governance Goes Wrong! London: Horn Heritage.

Duffield Mark (2001). Global Governance and the New Wars: The Merging of Development and Security. London: Zed Books.

Eachard, John (1996). Early Responses to Hobbes [5]: Mr. Hobb's State of Nature considered: In a Dialogue between Philautus and Timothy. Reprint of the 1672 ed. Early Responses to Hobbes. London: Routledge, Thoemmes.

Eisner, E. W. (1991). The Enlightened Eye: Qualitative Inquiry and the Enhancement of Educational Practice. New York: Macmillan.

Ellis, Stephen (1996). Africa Now: People, Policies & Institutions. The Hague: Ministry of Foreign Affairs (DGIS); London: J. Currey.

Fanthorpe, Richard (2001). Neither Citizen Nor Subject? Lumpen Agency and the Legacy of Native Administration in Sierra Leone. In: *African Affairs* 100 (2001).

Fanthorpe, Richard (2007). Sierra Leone: The Influence of the Secret Societies, with Special Reference to Female Genital Mutilation. <http://www.unhcr.org/cgi-bin/texis/vtx/refworld/rwmain?docid=46cee3152> Rev. 2009-03-15.

Ferme, Mariane C. (2001). The Underneath of Things: Violence, History, and the Everyday in Sierra Leone. Berkeley; London: University of California Press.

Fitz-Gerald, Ann M. (2004). Global Facilitation Network for Security Sector Reform (GFN-SSR). Shrivenham: Wellington Hall, Cranfield University.

Fontana, Andrea and James H. Frey (1998). Interviewing. in: Denzin, Norman K. and Yvonna Lincoln (eds.). Collecting and Interpreting Qualitative Materials. London: SAGE Publications.

Fowler, William (2005). Operation Barras: The SAS Rescue Mission Sierra Leone 2000. London: Cassell Military.

Francis, David J. (ed.) (2005). Civil Militia: Africa's Intractable Security Menace? Aldershot: Ashgate.

Francis, David J. (2006). Uniting Africa : Building Regional Peace and Security Systems. Aldershot: Ashgate.

Fyfe, Christopher T. (2003). A History of Sierra Leone. Reprint. CA: Textbook Publishers.

Garcia, Ed (1997). A Time of Hope and Transformation: Sierra Leone Peace Process Reports and Reflections. London: International Alert.
Gberie, Lansana (2005). A Dirty War in West Africa: The RUF and the Destruction of Sierra Leone. London: Hurst & Company.

Ginifer, Jeremy and Oliver Kaye (2004). Evaluation of the Conflict Prevention Pools: Sierra Leone. London: Dept. for International Development, Bradford University, Channel Research Ltd.

Glentworth, Garth (1976). <u>Education and Research in Public Administration in Africa.</u> In: African Affairs 75:299 (1976), pp. 265-266.

Glentworth, Garth (2002). <u>Post-Conflict Reconstruction: Key Issues in Governance.</u> London: DfID Governance Department.

Goodhand, Jonathon and David Hulme (1999). <u>From Wars to Complex Political Emergencies: Understanding Conflict and Peace Building in the New World Disorder.</u> In: Third World Quarterly 20:1 (1999), pp. 13-26.

Goodman, Allan E. and Sandra C. Bogard (eds.) (1992). <u>Making Peace: The United States and Conflict Resolution</u>. Boulder: Westview Press.

Gottschalk, Louis A. (1995). <u>Content Analysis of Verbal Behavior: New Findings and Clinical Applications.</u> Hillsdale, N.J.: Lawrence Erlbaum Associates Inc.

Grant, Patrick (2001). <u>Literature, Rhetoric, and Violence in Northern Ireland, 1968-98: Hardened to Death</u>. Houndmills, Basingstoke, Hampshire: Palgrave.

Grant, Reg (2002). <u>Conflict in Northern Ireland.</u> London: Hodder Wayland.

Griffiths, M. (1998). <u>Educational Research for Social Justice: Getting Off the Fence.</u> Buckingham: Open University Press.

Gutkind, Erwin A. (ed.) (1943). <u>Creative Demobilisation</u>. International Library of Sociology and Social Reconstruction. London: Kegan Paul, Trench, Trubner.

Hagman, Hans-Christian (1996). <u>UN-NATO Operational Co-operation in Peacekeeping 1992-1995.</u> London: Dept. of War Studies, King's College, University of London.

Harris, David (2002). <u>Post-Conflict Elections or Post-Elections Conflict: Sierra Leone 2002 and Patterns of Voting in Sub-Saharan Africa.</u> School of Oriental and African Studies, University of London.

Harvey, Colin (2005). <u>Catherine Phuong, The International Protection of Internally Displaced Persons.</u> In: International Journal of Refugee Law 17:4 (2005), pp. 823-827.

Harvey, Lee (1990). <u>Critical Social Research</u>. London: Unwin Hyman.

Hayward, Fred (1989). State Consolidation, Fragmentation and Decay. In: O'Brien, Donald Cruise, John Dunn and Richard Rathbone (eds.). West African States. 2nd ed. New York: Cambridge University Press.
Herbst, Jeffrey (1996). Responding to State Failure in Africa. In: International Security 21:3 (1996), pp.120-144.

Herbst, Jeffrey (2000). States and Power in Africa: Comparative Lessons in Authority and Control. Princeton, N.J.: Princeton University Press.

Hewitt, Vernon (1997). The New International Politics of South Asia. Manchester: Manchester University Press, pp. 83-106, 109-136.

Hirsch, John L. (2001). Sierra Leone: Diamonds and the Struggle for Democracy. Boulder, Colo.; London: Lynne Rienner Publishers.

Holm, Hans-Henrik (1998). The Responsibility That Will Not Go Away: Weak States in the International System. Paper presented at the Failed States Conference. West Lafayette: Purdue University, 25-27 February 1998.

Holm, Hans-Henrik (2001). A Disaggregated World Order in the Making: Policy Towards Failed States as an Example. In: International Politics 38:3 (2001), pp. 357-374.

Holm, Hans-Henrik (2002). Failing Failed States: Who Forgets the Forgotten? In: Security Dialogue 33:4 (2002), pp. 457-472.

Holsti, Kalevi J. (1996). The State, War, and the State of War. Cambridge; New York, N.Y.: Cambridge University Press.

Holzgrefe, Jeff L. and Robert O. Keohane (eds.) (2003). Humanitarian Intervention: Ethical, Legal and Political Dilemmas. Cambridge; New York: Cambridge University Press.

Hopkins, Nicholas S. (2007). Charisma and Responsibility: Max Weber, Kurt Eisner, and the Bavarian Revolution of 1918. In: Max Weber Studies 7:2 (2007), pp. 185-211.

Horton, Lynn (1964). After Democracy: Advances and Challenges for Women's Movements in Latin America. In: Latin American Politics & Society 49:1 (2007), pp. 165-176.

Human Rights Watch (2000). Sierra Leone: Recommendations to the International Contact Group on Sierra Leone. New York: AI Index: AFR

51/05/99, 19 April 1999; Amnesty International Report 2000: AI Index: POL 10/01/00.

Ignatieff, Michael (2002). Looking Forward - Intervention and State Failure. In: Dissent 49:1 (2002), pp. 115-123.

Ignatieff, Michael (2003). State Failure and Nation-Building. in: Holzgrefe, Jeff L. and Robert O. Keohane (eds.). Humanitarian Intervention: Ethical, Legal and Political Dilemmas. Cambridge; New York: Cambridge University Press.

International Crisis Group (2001). Sierra Leone: Managing Uncertainty. ICG Africa Report 35. Freetown/Brussels: International Crisis Group, 24 October 2001.

International Crisis Group (2002). Sierra Leone after Elections: Politics as Usual. ICG Africa Report 49. Freetown/Brussels: International Crisis Group, 12 July 2002.

International Crisis Group (2003). The State of Security and Governance. ICG Africa Report 67. Freetown/Brussels: International Crisis Group, 2 September 2003.

International Crisis Group (2004). Liberia and Sierra Leone: Rebuilding Failed States. ICG Africa Report 87. Freetown/Brussels: International Crisis Group, 8 December 2004.

IRIN (1998). IRIN-WA Weekly Roundup 34 of Main Events in West Africa covering the period (Friday) 30 January to (Thursday) 5 February 1998.

Jackson, Robert H. (1990). Quasi-States: Sovereignty, International Relations and the Third World. Cambridge: Cambridge University Press.

Jackson, Robert H. (1998). Surrogate Sovereignty?: Great Power Responsibility and 'Failed States'. Working Paper 25. Vancouver: Institute of International Relations, University of British Columbia.

Jackson, Robert H. and Carl G. Rosberg (1982). Why Africa's Weak States Persist: The Empirical and the Juridical in Statehood. In: World Politics 35:1 (1982), pp. 1-24.
Jett, Dannis (1999). Why Peacekeeping Fails. New York: Palgrave.

Kant, Immanuel. Perpetual Peace: A Philosophical Sketch.

Kaplan, Robert (1994). <u>The Coming Anarchy: How Scarcity, Crime, Overpopulation, Tribalism, and Disease are Rapidly Destroying the Social Fabric of Our Planet.</u> In: Atlantic Monthly 273 (1994), pp. 44-76.

Kaplan, Robert (1996). <u>The Ends of the Earth.</u> Part 1. New York: Random House.

Kaplan, Robert (2000). <u>The Coming Anarchy: Shattering the Dreams of the Post Cold War.</u> New York: Random House.

Kaplan, Robert (2001). <u>The Coming Anarchy: Shattering the Dreams of the Post-Cold War World</u>. Vintage Books USA.

King, Charles (1997). <u>Ending Civil Wars</u>. Adelphi Paper 308. International Institute for Strategic Studies. Oxford: Oxford University Press.

Krippendorff, K. (2004). <u>Content Analysis: An introduction to its methodology.</u> 2nd edition, Thousand Oaks, CA: Sage.

Kuhne, W. (2001). <u>From Peacekeeping to Postconflict Peacebuilding: Peacebuilding: A Field Guide.</u> London: Lynne Rienner Publishers.

Kumar, Krishna (1996). <u>Learning From Conflict</u>. London: Sangam.

Kumar, Krishna (1998). <u>Postconflict Elections, Democratization, and International Assistance</u>. Boulder; London: Lynne Rienner Publishers.

Kwabo, Nathaniel (2008). <u>On Robert H. Bates, When Things Fall Apart: State Failure in Late-Century Africa</u>. Cambridge: Cambridge University Press.

Lambourne, Wendy (2004). <u>Justice and Reconciliation: Postconflict Peacebuilding in Cambodia and Rwanda</u>. In: Abu-Nimer, Mohammed (ed.). Reconciliation, Justice, and Coexistence: Theory and Practice. New York: Lexington, pp. 311-337.

Leonard, Mark, Catherine Stead and Conrad Smewing (2002). <u>Public Diplomacy.</u> London: The Foreign Policy Center. Available from <www.fpc.org.uk> Rev. 2004-03-25.
Licklider, Roy (ed.) (1993). <u>Stopping the Killing: How Civil Wars End.</u> New York: New York University Press.

Luttwak, Edward (1987). <u>Strategy: The Logic of War and Peace.</u> Cambridge, Mass.: Belknap Press of Harvard University Press.

Luttwak Edward N. (1999). <u>Give War a Chance.</u> In: Foreign Affairs 78:4 (1999), pp. 36-44.

Luttwak, Edward N. (2002). <u>Strategy: The Logic of War and Peace</u>. Rev., enlarged ed. Cambridge, Mass.

Mair, Stefan (2008). <u>A New Approach: The Need to Focus on Failing States.</u> In: Harvard International Review 29:4 (2008), pp. 52-56.

Malan, Mark, Sarah Meek, Thokozani Thusi, Jeremy Ginifer and Patrick Coker (2003). <u>Sierra Leone: Building the Road to Recovery.</u> Monograph 80 (2003).

Marcus, Harold (1995). <u>John Sorenson, Imagining Ethiopia: Struggles for History and Identity in the Horn of Africa.</u> In: The Journal of African History 36:2 (1995), pp. 346-348.

McEvoy-Levy, Siobhán (2006). <u>Troublemakers or Peacemakers?: Youth and Post-Accord Peace Building</u>. Notre Dame, Ind.: University of Notre Dame Press.

Miall, Hugh (2005). <u>Understanding Contemporary Conflict.</u> In: Ramsbotham, Oliver, Tom Woodhouse and Hugh Miall. Contemporary Conflict Resolution. Cambridge: Polity Press.

Mill, John Stuart (1973). <u>A Few Words on Nonintervention</u>. In: Himmelfarb, Gertrude (ed.). Essays on Politics and Culture. Gloucester: Peter Smith, pp. 368-84.

Mill, John Stuart and John M. Robson (1999). <u>The Collected Works of John Stuart Mill.</u> 33 volumes. Toronto: University of Toronto Press, 1963-1991.

Moore, Karen, Chris Squire and Foday MacBailey (2003). <u>Sierra Leone National Recovery Strategy Assessment.</u> Final Report, 24 December. Freetown.

Morgan, E. Philip (1974). <u>The Administration of Change in Africa: Essays in the Theory and Practice of Development Administration in Africa.</u> New York: Dunellen.

Muana, Patrick K., Chris Corcoran and Russell D. Feingold (2005). Representations of Violence: Art about the Sierra Leone Civil War. Madison: 21st Century African Youth Movement.

Musah, Abdel-Fatau and Kayode Fayemi (2000). Mercenaries: An African Security Dilemma. London; Sterling, Va.: Pluto Press.

Neuendorf, Kimberly A. (2002). The content analysis guidebook. <http://academic.csuohio.edu/kneuendorf/content>.

Nkrumah, Kwame (1965). Neo-Colonialism: The Last Stage of Imperialism. London: Nelson.

Norton, Richard J. and James F. Miskel (1997). Spotting Trouble: Identifying Faltering and Failing States. In: Naval War College Review 50:2 (1997), pp. 79-91.

Nwokedi, Emeka (1992). Regional Integration and Regional Security: ECOMOG, Nigeria and the Liberian Crisis. Talence, France: Centre d'étude d'Afrique noire, Institut d'études politiques de Bordeaux.

Olonisakin, Funmi (2000). Reinventing Peacekeeping in Africa: Conceptual and Legal Issues in ECOMOG Operations. The Hague; Boston: Kluwer Law International.

Oludipe, Olayinka (2000). Sierra Leone : One Year After Lome. Centre for Democracy & Development.

Paris, Roland (1997). Peacebuilding and the Limits of Liberal Internationalism. In: International Security 22:2 (1997), pp. 54-89.

Paris, Roland (2001). Human Security: Paradigm Shift or Hot Air. In: International Security 26:2 (2001), pp. 87-102.

Pearsall, Judy (ed.) (1999). The Concise Oxford Dictionary. 10th ed. Oxford.

Perham, Margery (1962). The Colonial Reckoning. London: Collins.

Perham, Margery (1967). Colonial Sequence 1930 to 1949: A Chronological Commentary Upon British Colonial Policy Especially. London: Methuen.

Pha, Anna and Peter Seymor (2003). "Failed States" Doctrine. In: The Guardian, 6 August 2003. <http://www.cpa.org.au/garchve03/1149failed.html> Rev. 2009-03-15.

Pham, John-Peter (2005a). Democracy By Force?: Lessons from the Restoration of the State in Sierra Leone. In: Whitehead Journal of Diplomacy and International Relations 129 (2005).

Pham, John-Peter (2005b). Child Soldiers, Adult Interests: The Global Dimensions of the Sierra Leonean Tragedy. New York: Nova Science.

Pham, John-Peter (2006). The Sierra Leonean Tragedy: History and Global Dimensions. New York, N.Y.: Nova Science Publishers.

Phillips, Caryl (2003). Distant Voices. The Guardian, 19 July 2003. <http://www.guardian.co.uk/books/2003/jul/19/sierraleone.shopping> Rev. 2009-03-20.

Ramsbotham, Oliver, Tom Woodhouse and Hugh Miall (2005). Contemporary Conflict Resolution. 2nd ed. Cambridge, Malden: Polity Press.

Rehn, Elisabeth and Ellen Johnson Sirleaf (2002). Women, War, Peace: The Independent Experts' Assessment on the Impact of Armed Conflict on Women and Women's Role in Peace Building. New York, N.Y.: UNIFEM.

Reno, William (1995). Corruption and State Politics in Sierra Leone. Cambridge; New York: Cambridge University Press.

Reno, William (1998). Warlord Politics and African States. Boulder; London: Lynne Rienner Publishers.

Reno, William (2004). Order and Commerce in Turbulent Areas: 19th century Lessons, 21st Century Practice. In: Third World Quarterly 25:4 (2004), pp. 607-626.

Richards, Paul (1996). Fighting for the Rain Forest: War, Youth and Resources in Sierra Leone. Portsmouth, N.H: Heinemann.

Richards, Paul (2002). Fighting for the Rain Forest: War, Youth and Resources in Sierra Leone. 4. impr. Oxford: International African Inst.

Riley, Stephen P. (1996). Liberia and Sierra Leone: Anarchy or Peace in West Africa? Research Institute for the Study of Conflict and Terrorism.

Robson, Colin (1993). <u>Real World Research: A Resource for Social Scientists and Practitioner-Researchers.</u> Oxford; Cambridge, Mass.: Blackwell Publishers.

Rodney, Walter (1978). <u>How Europe Underdeveloped Africa.</u> London: Bogle-L'Ouverhure Publications.

Rotberg, Robert I. (2003). <u>State Failure and State Weakness in a Time of Terror.</u> Washington, D.C.: Brookings Institution Press.

Rotberg, Robert I. (2004). <u>When States Fail: Causes and Consequences.</u> Princeton, N.J.: Princeton University Press.

Rummel, R. J. (1983). <u>Libertarianism and International Violence.</u> In: Journal of Conflict Resolution 27 (1983).

Said, Edward (2003). <u>Orientalism 25 Years Later: Worldly Humanism v. the Empire-Builders.</u> A Counter Punch Special Report, 4 August 2003. <http://www.counterpunch.org/said08052003.html> Rev. 2009-03-15.

Samura, Abdulai (2009). <u>SIERRA LEONE: The Bondo Debate: An Affront to the Sierra Leonean Woman.</u> <http://www.fgmnetwork.org/gonews.php?subaction= showfull&id=1235133213&archive=> Rev. 2009-03-20.

Sandbrook, Richard (1996). <u>Transitions without Consolidation: Democratization in Six African Cases.</u> In: Third World Quarterly 17:1 (1996).

Schmitt, Carl (1996). <u>The Leviathan in the State Theory of Thomas Hobbes: Meaning and Failure of a Political Symbol.</u> Westport, Conn.: Greenwood Press.

Schumpeter, J. A. (1943). <u>Capitalism in the Postwar World.</u> In: Harris, S. E. (ed.). Postwar Economic Problems. New York, London: McGraw-Hill.

Simpson, J. A. and E. S. C. Weiner (ed.) (1989). <u>The Oxford English Dictionary.</u> 2nd ed. 20 Vol. Oxford.

Singer, Joel David and Melvin Small (1972). <u>The Wages of War, 1816-1965: A Statistical Handbook.</u> John Wiley & Sons.

Smillie, Ian (2000). <u>Getting to the Heart of the Matter: Sierra Leone, Diamonds, and Human Security.</u> In: Social Justice 27:4 (2000), pp. 24-31.

Smith, C.P., Atkinson, J.W., McClelland, D.C. and Veroff, J. (1992). <u>Mitigation and Personality:</u> Handbook of thematic content analysis. New York; Cambridge University Press.

Sorensen, George (1999). <u>Development in Fragile/Failed States.</u> Failed States Conference. West Lafayette: Purdue University, 7-11 April 1999.

Stedman, Stephen J. (1991). <u>Conflict and Conflict Resolution in Africa.</u> In: Deng, Francis M. and I. William Zartman (eds.). Conflict Resolution in Africa. Washington, D.C.: Brookings Institution.

Stedman, Stephen J. (2002). <u>Introduction.</u> In: Stedman, Stephen J., Donald Rothchild and Elizabeth M. Cousens (eds.). Ending Civil Wars: The Implementation of Peace Agreements. Boulder, Colo.: Lynne Rienner Publishers.

Stewart, Frances (2004). <u>Development and Security.</u> In: Centre for Defence Studies 4:3 (2004), pp. 261-288.

Stohl, Rachel J. (1998). <u>Deadly Rounds: Ammunition and Armed Conflict.</u> London: British American Security Information Council.

Stone, John (2007). <u>Clausewitz's Trinity and Contemporary Conflict.</u> In: Civil Wars 9:3 (2007), pp. 282-296.

Strayer, Joseph R. (1970). <u>On the Medieval Origins of the Modern State.</u> Princeton: Princeton University Press.

Talbot, Chris (2000). <u>Britain Steps Up Military Intervention in Sierra Leone.</u> BBC, 12 May 2000. <http://www.wsws.org/articles/2000/may2000/sier-m12.shtml> Rev. 2009-03-20.

The Children And Armed Conflict Unit. <u>Sierra Leone.</u> <http://www.essex.ac.uk/ armedcon/world/africa/west_africa/sierra_leone/default.htm> Rev. 2009-03-15.

Thompson, Brian (2007). <u>Sierra Leone: Reform or Relapse? Conflict and Governance Reform.</u> A Chatham House Report.

Thürer, Daniel (1999). The "Failed State" and International Law. In: International Review of the Red Cross No. 836, p. 731-761. <http://www.icrc.org/web/eng/ siteeng0.nsf/html/57JQ6U> Rev. 2009-03-17.

Tilly, Charles (1990). Coercion, Capital, and European States, A.D.990-1990. Oxford: Basil Blackwell.

Tilly, Charles (1992). Coercion, Capital, and European States, AD 990-1992. Cambridge, MA: Blackwell.

Tilly, Charles and Gabriel Ardant (1975). The Formation of National States in Western Europe. Princeton, N.J.: Princeton University Press.

Tilly, Charles, Peter B. Evans, Dietrich Rueschemeyer and Theda Skocpol (1987). War Making and State Making as Organized Crime. Cambridge: Cambridge University Press.

TRC. The Final Report of the Truth & Reconciliation Commission of Sierra Leone. CHAPTER TWO Governance, Volume 3A. Sierra Leone Truth & Reconciliation   Commission. <http://trcsierraleone.org/drwebsite/publish/v3a-c2.shtml> Rev. 2009-03-19.

United Nations (1992). General Assembly/Security Council, An Agenda for Peace: Preventive Diplomacy, Peacemaking and Peacekeeping 1992, A/47/277-S/24111,   17   June   1992. <http://www.un.org/Docs/SC/agpeace.html> Rev. 2009-09-19.

United Nations (1998). Security Council, S/RES/1181, 13 July 1998. <http://daccess-ods.un.org/TMP/5446621.html> Rev. 2009-03-15.

United Nations (1999a). Security Council, S/RES/1220, 12 January 1999. <http://daccess-ods.un.org/TMP/8765476.html> Rev. 2009-03-15.

United Nations (1999b). Security Council, S/RES/1231, 11 March 1999. <http://daccess-ods.un.org/TMP/1211416.html> Rev. 2009-03-15.
United Nations (2000). Security Council, Report of the Security Council mission   to   Sierra   Leone,   S/2000/992,   16   October   2000. <http://www.un.org/Depts/dpko/ unamsilscmission.pdf> Rev. 2009-03-19.

United Nations (2001). Security Council, S/RES/1346, 30 March 2001. <http://daccess-ods.un.org/TMP/4918088.html> Rev. 2009-03-19.

United Nations (2004). Security Council, Twenty-Fourth Report of the Secretary-General on the United Nations Mission in Sierra Leone, S/2004/965, 10 December 2004. <http://daccess-ods.un.org/TMP/2041603.html> Rev. 2009-03-15.

Von Lieres, Bettina (2002). Marginalisation and Politics in Post-Apartheid South Africa. University of Essex.

Wallensteen, Peter (1999). State Failure, Ethnocracy and Armed Conflict: Towards New Conceptions of Governance. Discussion paper, Failed States Conference II, Purdue University, 8-11 April 1999.

Wallensteen, Peter, and Carina Staibano (eds.) (2005). International Sanctions: Between Words and Wars in the Global System. London, New York: Frank Cass.

Weber, Max (1913/1968). Economy and Society: An Outline of Interpretive Sociology. Vol. 2, translated and edited by G. Roth and C. Wittich. New York: Bedminister Press.

Williams, John, Donald Sutherland, Kimberley Cartwright and Martin Byrnes (2002). Sierra Leone: Diamond Policy Study. Available at <http://www.dfid.gov.uk> Rev. 2009-03-20.

Wilson, James Q. (1989). Bureaucracy: What Government Agencies Do and Why They Do It. New York: Basic Books.

World Bank (2003). Sierra Leone—Strategic Options for Public Sector Reform. Report 25110-SL, 5 August 2003. Washington, D.C.: The World Bank.

Yarjah, Tamba (2000). Econometric Investigation Into Some Aspects of the Sierra Leone Economy. Reading: University of Reading.

Zack-Williams, Alfred B. (1985). Female Labour and Exploitation Within African Social Formations. In: Women in Nigeria Today, pp. 61-67.

Zack-Williams, Alfred B. (1999). Sierra Leone: The Political Economy of Civil War, 1991-98. In: Third World Quarterly 20:1 (1999), pp. 143-62.

Zartman, I. William (ed.) (1995a). <u>Collapsed States: The Disintegration and Restoration of Legitimate Authority.</u> Boulder; London: Lynne Rienner Publishers.

Zartman, I. William (ed.) (1995b). <u>Elusive Peace: Negotiating an End to Civil Wars.</u> Washington, D.C.: The Brookings Institution.

Zartman, I. William (2002). <u>Zerfall und Wiederherstellung legitimer staatlicher Strukturen.</u> In: Jahrbuch Menschenrechte, vol. 2002 (2001), pp. 17-27.

Zartman, I. William (2004). <u>Posing the Problem of State Collapse.</u> In: Zartman, I. William (ed.). Collapsed States: The Disintegration and Restoration of Legitimate Authority. Boulder: Lynne Rienner Publishers.

Zartman, I. William and Viktor A. Kremeni (2005). <u>Peace Versus Justice: Negotiating Forward - and Backward-Looking Outcomes.</u> Lanham, MD: Rowman & Littlefield.

Zinnes, Dina A. (1962). <u>Hostility in International Decision-Making.</u> In: Journal of Conflict Resolution 6:3 (1962), pp. 236-243.

www.ingramcontent.com/pod-product-compliance
Lightning Source LLC
Chambersburg PA
CBHW060312290526
45789CB00001B/495

9 781470 177805